BLOW OUT, YOU BUGLES

THE WAR SERVICE OF THREE ACOCKS GREEN FAMILIES

By

Conrad Lisk

www.songlome.com
Cover adapted by Sondiata Global Media Ltd
Photograph of St Mary the Virgin Church, Acocks
Green by Conrad Lisk.

ISBN-978-1-999787-81-3

Blow out, you bugles, over the rich Dead!
There's none of these so lonely and poor of old,
But, dying, has made us rarer gifts than gold.
These laid the world away; poured out the red
Sweet wine of youth; gave up the years to be
Of work and joy, and that unhoped serene,
That men call age; and those who would have been
Their sons, they gave, their immortality.

Rupert Brooke (1887 - 1915)

DEDICATION

To all men and women from Acocks Green
who made the ultimate sacrifice
during the 1939 – 1945 War.

ACKNOWLEDGEMENTS

Thanks to all those who helped in the preparation of this work. Especially to my wife and daughter who have been very tolerant of the amount of time I have spent in front of the computer screen, and my parents who infected me with the history bug from the start. Also, I thank the relatives of the fallen: Anthony Meades, Maureen Powell née Priest, Gordon Anthony Barber, and Susan Matheson née Helm, for all the information about their deceased family members. Thanks also to Georgina Sales, who helped me trace one of the living relatives. Appreciation also goes out to the officers and members of the Java Far East POW Association. Thanks also to Father Andrew Bullock and other officers of St Mary the Virgin church at Acocks Green - which plays a central part in this work. Finally, I am grateful to Khaday Mansaray for her invaluable support towards publication and Sqn Ldr Winston Forde RAF Ret'd who has acted as my Editor.

AUTHOR'S NOTE

The bulk of this work is set during World War Two, at a time when the map of the world was very different from today's. The largest country in the world was then the Soviet Union, which comprised present-day Russia and some of the countries which surround it, including Ukraine and Belarus. Present day Slovakia and the Czech Republic were then a single country, Czechoslovakia.

Many countries were ruled as colonies or territories of others. France and Britain had such possessions all over the world. Britain in particular, used many of its colonies as naval bases – such as Singapore, Sierra Leone, Gibraltar (now still a UK territory), and Malta. Britain's most prized colony - the 'jewel in her crown' - was India, which then included what are now Pakistan and Bangladesh. France ruled much of North Africa, including Morocco and Algeria. Italy had some colonies in Africa, including Libya and much of Somalia. Japan had many possessions on the Asian mainland and also in the Pacific.

INTRODUCTION

Acocks Green is a suburb of Birmingham.[1] It first developed north of the current centre at the roundabout where the Warwick Road meets Shirley and Westley Roads. Hyron Hall and Broom Hall were moated manor houses located in the area. During the end of the 18th century, the Warwick and Birmingham Canal was cut through Acocks' Green. This resulted in wharfs being constructed at Stockfield Road and Yardley Road. The increased prosperity brought by the canal prompted the construction of farms and large residences.

The village began to expand in the 19th century when it was connected to the Birmingham to Oxford railway in 1852. At this time there were three hamlets along the Warwick Road; Flint Green, Acocks Green, and Westley Brook. Westley Brook was to become the centre of modern Acocks Green. As Acocks Green was closer to the station, it developed faster than the old centre.

In 1911, Yardley, of which Acocks Green was a part of, was absorbed into Birmingham. Birmingham was in need of housing and in the mid-1920s, municipal housing was built on around half of Acocks Green, resulting in a large increase in the population. Acocks Green benefited from an increase in commerce brought

---

[1] 'Acocks Green' by Michael Byrne (1997) The History Press.

about by the newcomers. It developed into a major shopping area and churches and meeting halls were extended to accommodate more people.

The suburb has flourished ever since, although industries which existed there in the mid-twentieth century have closed. It boasts a considerable shopping parade along the Warwick Road. Its centre is a former tram terminus, now the roundabout at the junction of Shirley Road, Warwick Road, and Westley Road. The roundabout is grassed over and known as 'the Green.' Acocks

Having set the scene, I turn to the story behind this work. I moved into Acocks Green many years ago. One Sunday, a few weeks after my arrival, I went to a service at the local parish church, St Mary The Virgin, which is not far from 'the Green'.

As is the case with many older churches, people had been buried in the churchyard until fairly recently. Walking up the hill to the church building I could see gravestones on either side of the path. To the right hand side as I went up the hill, was a distinctive Commonwealth War Graves Commission headstone.

I am familiar with such gravestones, having seen them in war cemeteries in many countries overseas. However, this was the first time I had ever seen one in the UK. Perhaps we tend to think of our war dead as having shed their blood abroad, and historically they would be buried where they fell. I wondered about the deceased service person – who they had been, what was their cause of death, and so on. As I rounded the corner towards the church entrance, I caught sight of two more such gravestones.

Further examination of the three indicated that one also commemorated a person described as 'lost at sea.'

I wondered about the history of the dead persons. I wondered about their relatives - siblings, spouses, children, or parents – who they may have left behind.

As the years passed, I decided to research these matters. I would look not only into the lives of the people buried, or commemorated, but also those of any relatives who also served in the war. In addition, I would also look into the lives of their other family members, as best as possible.

Many discoveries awaited me. Not only about the lives and deaths of those buried, or commemorated in the churchyard, but also about their relatives and about aspects of the war and earlier history which I had previously known little about.

This work, therefore, covers the lives of the men from three local families, who served in the war – those who lived and those who died. It also follows the lives, post-war, of the survivors and the next of kin of the dead. By way of context, the course of the war is covered in some detail, in places all over the world, but especially in Birmingham and in the areas where our subjects served.

TABLE OF CONTENTS

Chapter One: Early Days

The Barber, Helm and Priest families all feature in the 1911 census, the first to be filled out by the heads of family, rather than by the census enumerators as previously.

Interestingly, none of the three families were in Birmingham in 1911. Two of them then lived in the nearby Black Country.

The Barber family lived at 22 Bromford Lane, West Bromwich, then in Staffordshire. The father Sidney George Barber who I shall call 'Sidney', was aged forty-two, and is noted as a labourer of the local authority of West Bromwich commonly known as the corporation. His wife, Annie Barber née Burrows, was twenty-nine and gave no occupation – she was presumably a housewife. They had been married for seven years.

At that time they had two children, a daughter aged five, named as 'Nellie,' who appears on the official records as 'Rose Valerie Barber' so I shall refer to her as 'Valerie' and a son aged two, named as 'Baizle,' which seems to be a phonetic spelling of 'Basil.' The son, Sidney Basil Barber alias 'Basil' had been born on 10 December 1908.

The Priest family lived at 37 Olive Road, Halesowen, then in Worcestershire. The father, 'Frederick Senior' was twenty-eight years old. He was described in the census as a warehouse-man at a tube works, an industry which survived in the area until relatively recently. His marriage certificate indicates that his own father had also been a tube worker. His wife, Elsie Gwendola Priest, née Williams was aged twenty-seven, and was presumably, a housewife; they had married five years before. At the time they had a son, Frederick Charles Priest aged five years, 'Frederick Junior,' born on 29 November 1905. They also had a young daughter called Dorothy Dinah Priest, aged about one year.

The Helm family did not live in the West Midlands at the time. The father, William Frederick Helm lived in Hampshire. His address was Victoria Inn, Victoria Road, Woolston. He was single, his occupation was listed as 'surveyor' and his age as twenty-six. The head of the household was his widowed mother Ellen Helm, aged sixty-seven, who was noted as a 'licensed victualler' and ran a public house. Three schoolchildren were listed at the address, and also a domestic servant. The Inn is recorded as having ten rooms. William had been born in the same area in 1884.

Over the next few years there would be changes to all the families. The Priests had another daughter on 30 October 1912, but sadly, the girl, Bertha, died a few days later. On 16 October 1913, another son arrived, Alfred Lewis Priest known to the family as 'Alf'. He was apparently named after his maternal grandfather, Alfred Lewis Williams, who had been living with the family in 1911 at the time of the census.

The Barbers also had another child, a daughter, Christine, born in 1912.

All the families were caught up in the upheaval of the First World War, the 'Great War' that broke out in the summer of 1914. By now both the Barber and Priest families lived in Birmingham. Their fathers sought to enlist in the forces.

Sidney George Barber had some previous part-time military experience as a member of the local militia. Pictures of him sitting with his family, wearing a militia uniform would suggest that he, may have been an officer. However, Sidney's attempts to enlist during the First World War met with limited success.   In quick succession he joined, the regiments of the Oxfordshire and Buckinghamshire Light Infantry followed by the Durham Light Infantry. On each occasion he got discharged after a short while on the grounds that he 'was not likely to become an efficient soldier.' Sidney would have been aged forty-five at the start of the War. Although he gave his age as thirty-eight each time he joined, he was deemed unsuitable for military service. In his army enlistment documents his occupation is given as 'tailor'.

Frederick Priest Snr held a job as a tram conductor at the time. He enlisted in the Royal Army Medical Corps.

William Frederick Helm joined the Royal Engineers in mid-1915. His service records include a letter from a previous employer recommending him to the military authorities. He married Ethel Victoria Robinson, also from Hampshire, later that year. He was to rise to the rank of Staff Sergeant and temporary Warrant Officer. His service records indicate that he was stationed at, or near Calais in France.

W F HELM IN UNIFORM AS A SERGEANT IN
THE ROYAL ENGINEERS
(Susan Matheson)

Birmingham suffered from the effects of the war in the same way as other towns and cities. Local regiments were formed and went into battle, mostly in France and Belgium, suffering heavy casualties. Telegram delivery boys would bring the terse notifications of bad news to the service persons' relatives. Industrial production largely shifted to war munitions. Women took up work previously done by men who had joined the forces.

Whilst Britain's towns and cities were normally safe due to the country's position as an island, this was the first conflict in which danger came from the air. Germany struck at Britain using its airships, called 'Zeppelins' in Britain although that company did not make all of the aircraft in question.

The attacks started in Norfolk in January 1915 and swiftly moved on to London. However, in 1916 the Midlands were affected. Two German airships apparently mistook the region for the North West, and bombed Tipton, Walsall and other towns in the Black Country, believing they were over Liverpool. At least thirty-six people were killed in the raid, or subsequently of their injuries. The Mayoress of Walsall was one of those to die afterwards. [2]

Birmingham escaped major air raids in this war. This may well have been due to regulations issued by the Chief Constable at the start of the conflict, restricting the use of outdoor lights at night, thus creating a blackout. An air raid on 19 October 1917 hit the Austin factory at Longbridge, which had been carelessly left lit. Lastly, another attempt to hit the city occurred on 12 April 1918, when German airships, unable to locate the city in the blackout, dropped their bombs over Hall Green, much of which was then open countryside. These attacks caused slight damage, but only a few injuries.

------

[2]*Birmingham In The First World War by J P Lehtbridge, Newgate Press.*

Each of our three families had a son born to them during the conflict, all of whom were destined to serve in the Second World War.

The first was Douglas Eric Priest known as 'Eric', born on 30 March 1917 at the Priests' house in Moilliett Street, Birmingham. This was near the Dudley Road in Winson Green, it seems to have been renamed subsequently. Frederick Snr was the informant, so he must have been serving in Britain, or on leave here.

Afterwards, on 23 October 1917, a son, Gordon Grant Helm was born at Newport, Isle of Wight, to the Helm family. His mother Ethel registered the birth, so it may be that William was serving abroad, or otherwise unavailable due to his military duties at the time.

Lastly, Dennis William Barber was born to the Barbers on 5 May 1918, at the family's residence at Cardigan Street in the city centre. Sidney's occupation is given as 'labourer in motor works,' so it would seem that he had given up trying to join the military, and was contributing to the war effort in that way instead.

The war ended in November 1918, happily with all the fathers still alive. In the aftermath of hostilities, there were yet more arrivals.

On 30 December 1921, another son, Herman Grant Helm, was born at James Street, Newport, Isle of Wight, to the Helm family. By then, the family address was given on the certificate as 118 New Avenue (most of which is now just 'The Avenue') in Acocks Green, Birmingham. William's occupation was still listed as 'surveyor'. Presumably family matters, or health reasons, had temporarily taken the family down south again. Herman would always be known to his family by his correct name, however due to the unpopularity of German names at the time (and later), he was more commonly known as 'Harry' and will be called that from now on.[3]

The Priest family had two more sons in quick succession. Alexander Howard Priest, known as 'Alec,' was born on 9 July 1920. The family still lived at Moilliett Street and Frederick Senior was still noted as being a tram conductor. Less than two years later, Vernon Leslie Priest known as 'Leslie' was born on 19 May 1922, all the family details being as stated above.

Basil Barber joined the Carrs Lane Scout Group, becoming a 'King Scout.' He was also awarded a swastika badge.[4] At the time this emblem was popular in Western cultures, de-

---

[3] Personal communication from Susan Matheson, July 2017.

[4] Personal communication from Gordon Anthony Barber, December 2014

spite its Eastern origins, but its significance was to change in the years to come.

In 1923, Basil received a high distinction whilst working as a delivery boy. He was selected to collect newspapers from New Street Station and deliver them to Castle Bromwich Hall for visiting royalty – Queen Alexandra, the then Queen Mother. For this, he later received a certificate of appreciation from Buckingham Palace.

In 1927, tragedy struck his family. Sidney George Barber passed away on 12 April, at the City Sanatorium at Yardley, from tuberculosis. The death certificate indicates that the family was then still living at Cardigan Street.

By 1930, they lived at Hattersley Grove in Acocks Green, Basil and his mother appeared on the electoral roll there. They were later to move to Fenton Road, also in Acocks Green.

In 1933, Valerie married David Peircey in Hendon, Middlesex. Later that year, they had a son, Dennis; sadly, David passed away within three years thereafter. In the same year, Christine Barber married Arthur Botherway at St Mary the Virgin church in Acocks's Green. They were to have a daughter four years later.

On 1 June 1936, Basil got married to Gladys May Nicholas, also at St Mary The Virgin Church,

Acocks Green. Gladys was the daughter of a confectioner's assistant. Dennis Barber was one of the witnesses to the wedding. At the time of his wedding, Basil's occupation was recorded as 'despatch clerk.' He went on to be employed by Prudential Assurance Co Ltd, at their Acocks Green office, as an insurance agent.

Gladys' address was given as Warwick Road, Acocks Green. The couple were to make their home there subsequently - the electoral roll for 1939 records them as both living in that same house. Basil's mother Anna was recorded as still living at Fenton Street. Dennis, who was twenty-one and just old enough to be recorded on the roll, was also recorded as living there.

The decade also saw weddings in the Priest family. On 28 October 1934, Frederick Priest Junior, now a butcher, married Norah Robinson, a shirt-maker. The wedding took place at St Oswald's Church, Bordesley Green. Frederick Junior's address was in Charles Road, Small Heath. Frederick Senior's name is down as the father of the groom, his job description now being 'tram stall man.'

One of the witnesses at the wedding was Eric John Meades. A few years later, on 29 March 1937, Eric John, described as a saw mill worker, married Frederick Junior's sister Dinah, described as a warehouse hand, at St Benedict's Church, Bordesley.

Both marriages were swiftly blessed with children, Maureen Avice Priest being born to Frederick Junior and Norah in 1937, and Anthony Eric Meades being born to Eric John and Dinah in 1938.

Alf Priest, then employed as a driver, joined the Territorial Army in the mid-1930s. This was the successor to the old militia, and the equivalent of today's Army Reserve, involving men in civilian life who did part-time military training and exercises. He served with the 5th Battalion of the Royal Warwickshire Regiment from 1931 to 1935. His brother Eric also worked as a driver, but did not join the Territorials.

In the mid-1920s the Helm family lived at Alexander Road in Acocks Green. Both William and Ethel appear on the electoral roll, at least up to 1935.

In the following years they moved to the adjacent street, Douglas Road. Sadly, on 1 February 1938, Ethel Helm passed away at the Birmingham General Hospital (now the Children's Hospital) at Steelhouse Lane, Birmingham. She had suffered a pulmonary embolism and other complications following an appendix operation.

The family next appear on the electoral roll at Douglas Road in 1939. Gordon, who turned twenty-one that year, appeared on the roll with his father. Perhaps Harry lived there as well but was too young to be recorded. Gordon is reported to have worked as a departmental manager at a fancy linen manufacturers, referred to as a 'buyer of fabrics,' I have no details of his employer. Harry worked for the Austin Motor Company.

In the early to mid-1930s, storm clouds gathered. Benito Mussolini's Fascist Party had seized power in Italy in the early 1920s, and Adolf Hitler's Nazi Party now did likewise in Germany. The swastika, which as we had seen was given as a Scout badge at this time, now became better known as the emblem of the Nazi party. Both Italy and Germany became dictatorships, with the governments detaining their opponents without trial. In Germany, Jewish people were also persecuted, being barred from the professions, having much of their property seized, and being detained in the growing network of concentration camps.

Later in the decade, Italy invaded Abyssinia (Ethiopia), and Germany and Italy intervened in the Spanish Civil War, supporting Nationalist army officers in their rebellion against the republican government. Japan invaded China, its soldiers committing atrocities at Nanjing which shocked the world. Members of the British public who may not have paid a great deal of attention events in these far-off lands, later held their breath as the prime minister – a Birmingham MP, Neville Chamberlain - flew to Munich in Germany to meet Hitler, and hopefully come to an agreement, which would stave off the prospect of a war arising from Germany's attempts to occupy Czechoslovakia. An agreement was reached between Germany on the one hand and Britain and France on the other. While Britain and France acquiesced in Germany's takeover of Czechoslovakia, Germany undertook not to seek any more territory in Europe.

The agreement reached at Munich served to delay the conflict only for a year, or so. Chamberlain's government reluctantly re-armed the country, particularly seeking to make many more modern fighter aircraft for the air force. In the summer of 1939, with war looming, the British government passed the Military Training Act, which provided for a form of peacetime conscription. Single men aged between twenty and twenty-two were to be called up into a militia, rather than the army. They would be given six months of basic training and then discharged into an actual reserve unit.

Before this scheme could take effect, it was overtaken by events. Germany invaded Poland on 1 September 1939. Britain and France de-clared war on Germany two days later.   World War II had begun.

Chapter Two: World War II - The Opening Rounds

On the day that the Second World War broke out, Parliament passed the National Service (Armed Forces) Act 1939. This introduced full conscription on males between the ages of eighteen and forty-one, superseding the previous scheme. Men were to be called up in various age groups, rather than all at once. Some workers deemed essential to the war effort, including miners, fishermen and slaughter men were deemed to be in 'reserved occupations' and exempt from conscription.

Those countries that had been Britain's colonies and were now independent, but still retained King George VI as their head of state were known as 'The 'Dominions' of the British Commonwealth, declared war on Germany in turn. New Zealand and Australia did so immediately, followed by South Africa and Canada shortly afterwards. Ireland though part of the Commonwealth and, therefore, officially still a 'Dominion,' remained neutral.

Britain's war started, as had the previous one, with a British Expeditionary Force being sent to France within weeks. In October 1939, men aged between 20 and 23 were required to enlist, being given the choice between the army, navy, or air force. The Priest family takes pride in the memory that all of the brothers who served in the second World War had volunteered rather than being conscripted. This can clearly be seen as Eric and Alf enlisted at Birmingham, the former on 19 September, and the latter on 21 October 1939, although both were older than those being called up at the time. Eric John Meades, their brother in law, was found to be medically unsuited to military service.[5] Frederick Junior, as a butcher, would have been considered a 'slaughter man' and treated as exempt from being called-up.

In line with their peacetime occupation, Alf and Eric joined as drivers, and were assigned to the Royal Army Service Corps ('RASC'). This unit mainly provided drivers to ambulance units, artillery batteries and others, among other duties. Both men held the rank of 'Driver,' an RASC equivalent of 'Private.' Officially they were in the Territorial Army, but this was now a full time outfit rather than one comprising part time soldiers known as 'weekend warriors' as it had been before the war. Volunteers and conscripts alike joined the Territorial Army rather than the regulars, because they would be demobilised as soon as the war ended. Alternatively, if they enlisted in the regular army they would be joining for a fixed period of time that could extend for some years after the war had ended.

Both were to serve in the British Expeditionary Force ('BEF'). Eric who, it will be remembered, did not have previous military experience was shipped out to France on 18 October 1939, not quite a month after he enlisted. He embarked at Southampton on that day, and arrived at Cherbourg in France a day later. He was attached to 5 Mobile Ambulance Company. On the other hand, Alf did not deploy abroad at this stage in spite of his Territorial Army experience. Rather, on 30 November 1939, he was assigned to 501 (Ammunition) Company RASC, at Home in the UK.

The conflict soon entered a period of time known as the 'Phoney War,' during which very little action took place on the front between British and French soldiers on the one side and the Germans on the other.

However, it could not be said that no fighting at all was taking place. The day after war was declared, RAF bomber aircraft struck at German warships at Wilhelmshaven and Cuxhaven. Six weeks later, Germany's air force, the *Luftwaffe* launched a raid on British warships at Rosyth. A German submarine operating as a 'U-boat' sank the British merchant ship *Athenia* in the Irish

Sea on the first day of the war. More daringly, another U-boat sank the British battleship *Royal Oak* in the waters of the supposedly-safe naval base at Scapa Flow, on 14 October 1939 resulting together in a heavy loss of life; 128 died on *Athenia* and 838 on the *Royal Oak*. Many of those killed on the battleship were boy sailors aged between fifteen and seventeen.

Christmas 1939 was a special time for the whole country. Those old enough probably reflected on the memorable euphoria during the First World War, when people thought and prayed that the fighting would be over by Christmas.

King George VI, in his Christmas broadcast, captured the nation's spirit of cautious optimism. In particular, he praised the armed forces, with special mention of the Royal Navy and Merchant Navy already engaged in maritime action across the Atlantic Ocean, expressing faith that the British army would likewise acquit itself well. In conclusion he quoted from a poem called 'God Knows,' then thought to be anonymous but now known to be by Minnie Louise Haskins:

'And I said to the man who stood at the gate of the year:
"Give me a light that I may tread safely

into the unknown."

And he replied:

"Go out into the darkness and put your hand into the Hand of God.

That shall be to you better than light and safer than a known way."

So I went forth, and finding the Hand of God, trod gladly into the night.

And He led me towards the hills and the breaking of day in the lone East.'

On 14 January 1940 Dennis Barber enlisted in the Royal Air Force (RAF), signing up at the former airship base of Cardington, in Bedfordshire, which was then being used as an RAF Recruitment Centre. A few days later he was sent to another recruitment centre at Morecambe, and then temporarily released back into civilian life for a few weeks. He joined the RAF Elementary Training School at Cranwell, Lincolnshire on 8 March 1940. He later continued his training at RAF Wilmslow in May as a trainee airman holding the rank of Aircraftman Class 2. Dennis served in the Royal Air Force Volunteer Reserve, the Air Force's equivalent of the Territorial Army, as did all of our subjects who joined the Air Force. Again, this had the advantage that should they survive the hostilities, they could be demobilised fairly soon, instead of having signed for a fixed, lengthy period of time.

Still in March, Eric Priest was granted ten days' leave to the UK, showing, perhaps, how relaxed the situation apparently was on the Front at that time.

The following month, Gordon Helm enlisted in the Royal Army Pay Corps ('RAPC') on 2 April 1940, apparently at Shrewsbury, as a Private and then posted to the main RAPC establishment at Leicester.

A few days later, ground warfare started in Europe, although not in France. Germany invaded Denmark and Norway on 9 April 1940. Denmark surrendered hours later, and the Norwegian capital Oslo fell within days. But Norway fought on, its forces retreating towards the north of the country and later receiving the support of British, French and exiled Polish army, air force and naval units.

Allied forces were to win victories over German forces, taking away their growing state of invincibility. In particular, German naval losses were high.

Shortly afterwards, Alf Priest was deployed across the English Channel into France. He left England on 10 April and arrived in France the following day, presumably still with 501 Ammunition Company RASC.

The Phoney War did not last very much longer. On 10 May 1940, German forces invaded Belgium, the Netherlands and Luxembourg, overrunning those countries by the end of the month. By so doing they were able to bypass France's Maginot Line fortifications running along the French/German border and set up after the 1919 Treaty of Versailles to ensure France should never have to suffer the catastrophes of World War One. In the event, this became a military liability when the Germans attacked France in the Spring of 1940 using blitzkrieg, a tactic that completely emasculated the Maginot Line's purpose. German troops thus entered northern France and faced the British Expeditionary Force, which had not yet had time to dig itself in owing to the speed of the attack. Also on 10 May, Neville Chamberlain resigned as Prime Minister to be replaced by Winston Churchill, the Minister in charge of the Royal Navy.

In due course, Allied forces in Norway would be withdrawn and redeployed and the country was finally fully occupied by Germany. The Norwegian royal family, its government and much of its armed forces came over to Britain to continue the struggle from these shores.

Within a matter of weeks British and French forces in France were defeated and in retreat, outfought by Germany's combination of infantry, heavy tanks and close air support. Many troops of both nations were captured by German forces, but the bulk of the British forces headed towards the port of Dunkirk on the north French coast. Between 26 May and 4 June 1940, hundreds of thousands of British, French and Belgian forces were evacuated to the UK from Dunkirk and other ports, in the face of German attacks by land and air. The Dunkirk evacuation is famed for the involvement of many small civilian boats whose crews answered the government's call to help rescue the British and other allied soldiers.

On 22 June 1940, the new French government led by Marshall Pétain, signed an armistice with Nazi Germany. Northern France remained under German occupation while southern France was governed by Petain's government, based at the spa town of Vichy. However, a few days before the armistice, a French Army brigadier and deputy minister, Charles de Gaulle, had broadcast from London calling upon French people to continue to resist. He became leader of the Free French forces, which continued the fight against Germany and her allies. The Vichy government treated him as a criminal and sentenced him to death in his absence. The two rival French authorities will feature later on.

BRITISH SOLDIERS WADE TO A SHIP DURING THE
EVACUATION FROM DUNKIRK
(IWM, under licence)

Fortunately, both Alf and Eric Priest were among the soldiers who returned home safely. Eric is recorded as having left France on 24 May 1940, just before the evacuation proper started. Alf's exact evacuation date is less precise, but took place sometime between 25 May and 5 June.

After the evacuation, Britain prepared for an enemy invasion and possible heavy air raids. Fear of invasion had been running for a few weeks already. On 14 May the War Secretary, Anthony Eden, made a radio broadcast calling on men between the ages of seventeen and sixty-five wishing to take part in the defence of the country from invasion, to report at their police stations to join the Local Defence Volunteers (LDV).

As most able-bodied men of military age were already in the forces, the LDV attracted men who were either too young, or too old to serve in the regular armed forces. Also, men in reserved occupations could volunteer too. Frederick Jr., as we have seen, was exempt from conscription, but could join the LDV and did so.

FREDERICK PRIEST Jr IN HOME GUARD UNIFORM
(Maureen Powell)

The Volunteers started off with no uniforms other than armbands marked 'LDV'. In addition they had no weapons issued to them. Recruits attended with what weapons they could lay hands on – including pitchforks, cudgels, shotguns, and Great War souvenir firearms. Within months they would be renamed the 'Home Guard', given army uniforms and issued proper weapons. They were to maintain a watch against invasion until long after that threat had receded.

The youngest of the Priest brothers, Leslie, joined the RAF, enlisting at the recruitment centre at Blackpool on 27 May 1940. He would go on to be stationed successively at two Bomber Command bases in Norfolk later in the year, RAF West Raynham and RAF Swinton Morley.

Meanwhile, the war came to Birmingham. This time a blackout was in force throughout the whole country, by order of central government.

The city experienced air raids during August, a month before similar attacks started in London. The first was on 9 August, when a sole German bomber dropped bombs on Erdington. Vivian Ronald James Fry, an eighteen-year old cinema operator, was killed when their family home was hit, becoming the city's first air raid fatality in any conflict. Other members of the family were injured.[6] Vivian's death certificate, issued three days afterwards, tersely gave his cause of death as 'due to war operations,' a line that was to be repeated in hundreds of other such certificates in the coming months and years.

Less than a week later, the *Luftwaffe* returned, attacking the Spitfire factory at Castle Bromwich (possibly the intended target for the first raid), causing some damage and thirteen deaths. Acocks Green was hit on the night of the 15th/16th August 1940, with two adult sisters killed when their house at Cottesbrook Road was hit. The suburb suffered another family tragedy later in the month, when four members of the Prince family – the parents and two children aged twelve and thirteen – were killed on the night of 24/25 August when a bomb fell on their house on Wildfell Road. Two other children survived.

That summer, RAF fighter aircraft fought the Luftwaffe for the skies over the UK, in what became known as the Battle of Britain. Germany hoped to destroy the RAF fighters and their bases and thus achieve air superiority, which

---

6 Swanhurst School project.BARRA website. This is an invaluable resource on the day to day incidents and casualties during the Birmingham Blitz. http://www.birminghamairraids.co.uk

would enable the proposed invasion. The German bombers and fighters were defeated by October, and the planned invasion postponed indefinitely. The fighter pilots were the heroes of the hour. The Prime Minster, speaking of them, famously said 'Never in the field of human conflict has so much been owed by so many to so few.' However, the bombing of London, and other British cities started towards the end of the Battle of Britain and continued afterwards, mostly by night. The air attacks would be known as 'the Blitz.'

Leicester, where the Royal Army Pay Corps had its main offices and where Gordon Helm was based, was not expected to be a major target of the bombing. In fact, evacuees were sent there from London to escape from air raids. Most of the Pay Corps soldiers were billeted in lodgings in the city, rather than living in barracks. However, the city suffered a major attack on the night of 19 November 1940. Sadly on that night, twelve Pay Corps soldiers died when their lodgings were destroyed by a bomb.[7]

Alec, the last of the Priest brothers to enlist, joined the RAF on 10 September 1940, also at Cardington. He was placed on the reserve list and released back into civilian life until recalled

_____

7 Jewish Gilroes website - http://www.jewish-gilroes.org.uk

on 10 December 1940, when he reported at the recruitment centre at Blackpool and was later assigned to No 20 (Training) Group, part of the Technical Training Command.

British soldiers were soon in action on land once again. This was the result of Italy entering the war on 11 June 1940, during the last days of the French campaign. On 27 September 1940, Fascist Italy, Nazi German and the Empire of Japan, signed a formal Tripartite Agreement in Berlin Germany as the three major States within the alliance comprising states opposed to the Allies comprising the Axis Powers. Within days British troops in Egypt had entered Italy's colonies in Libya, capturing Fort Capuzzo near the border between Egypt and Libya.

RAF squadrons flew ground-attack missions in support of British troops on operations. One such Unit being No. 211 Squadron, based at RAF Ismailia in Egypt. However, in late October 1940 when Italy attacked Greece from Albania, the British Command decided to support the Greek military by sending air support and some ground troops. Accordingly, No. 211 Squadron and other units were sent to Greece.

Dennis Barber, by now a Leading Aircraftman (LAC), was recorded as a serving member of No. 211 Squadron in Egypt as of 11 November 1940. He had by now completed his training as an equipment assistant, with responsibility for managing Supply stores. By 24 December he was with the squadron at Tatoi in Greece, an airfield near the town of Menidi in the northern outskirts of Athens. The squadron would later move to Paramythia, near the north-western border with Albania. Greek soldiers, with this air support on hand, were successful in holding back the Italian attackers.

A few days before that, Alf Priest had set off to war, once again. He embarked for the Middle East on 16 December 1940, now apparently with a heavy anti-aircraft artillery unit.

By that time German and Italian aircraft were menacing the British territories of Gibraltar and Malta in the Mediterranean Sea, and attacking British shipping. Convoys of British ships taking troops and supplies to Egypt, went the long way - around the Cape of Good Hope and up the Indian Ocean coast of Africa, to the Suez Canal. Alf's journey to Egypt was to take him two months.

All's journey to Egypt lasted for two months-From his travel dates, it seems that Alf travelled on Convoy WS5A, a convoy of twenty or so merchant ships and troopships with their destroyer and cruiser escorts.[8] These ships left Liverpool and the Clyde in mid-December, and headed south towards Africa.

The sea voyage was to give Alf yet more experience of combat, to add to anything he may have witnessed in France before and during the evacuation. On the night of Christmas Eve, the convoy was attacked off the Canary Islands by the German battle cruiser *Admiral Hipper*.[9] The German cruiser opened fire on the troopships damaging one, the *Empire Trooper.* The *Hipper* later withdrew, after exchanging fire with the escort cruiser *HMS Berwick.* The latter was damaged and four Royal Marines on board were killed. *Hipper* headed for Brest in occupied France, being low on fuel. It is not known which ship Alf was on, but as *Hipper* was firing with her main guns it is highly likely that many of the soldiers and sailors in the convoy would have been able to hear, if not see, the attack on the *Empire Trooper* and the subsequent battle between *Hipper* and *Berwick.*

8   **ROUTE TO THE EAST - the WS (Winston's Special) CONVOYS** by the late Arnold Hague, Lieutenant Commander, RNR (Rtd) (c) 2007(online at http://www.naval-history.net/xAH-WSConvoys01.htm).

9   Chronology of the War at Sea, 1939–1945: The Naval History of World War Two, Jürgen Rohwer, (2005), Annapolis: US Naval Institute Press.

THE ADMIRAL HIPPER
(Bundesarchiv)

HMS BERWICK
(Crown Copyright [public domain]).

The convoy proceeded on its way, most of its ships arriving at Freetown, Sierra Leone on 6 January 1941, and leaving there two days later. They arrived at Durban, South Africa a little over two weeks subsequently, and left after a few days there, to stop at Mombasa in Kenya and then proceeding via Aden to Suez in Egypt.

Alf disembarked at Egypt on 16 February 1941. He was still attached to a heavy anti-aircraft artillery unit. Two months later he was transferred to 173 Field Ambulance, and served with that Unit mainly for the rest of his military career. Incidentally, just weeks before Alf's arrival in Egypt, the conflict in North Africa had changed significantly. Germany had sent soldiers of its *Afrika Korps* to the region to assist the Italian forces against the Allies.

In the meantime in Birmingham, air raids had continued and worsened. The sufferings of people in London were generally known by the public, through newspaper and radio reports. However, this was not so for Birmingham. The censors insisted that Birmingham would normally only be known in reports of bomb damage, or deaths, as 'a Midlands town/city.' This was for fear of letting the German authorities know how successful, or otherwise their strikes on the city were, as it was a key industrial centre.[10]

Between 25 and 30 October 1940 the city centre was severely affected by air raids. Birm-

---

[10] *The Blitz: The British Under Attack (2010)* by Judith Gardiner

ingham University, the Art Gallery, Museum and the Town Hall, all suffered extensive damage. St Philip's Cathedral was damaged by fire, as was the roof of the City Council building. On 14 November 1940, the city centre of nearby Coventry was largely destroyed in an intensive German air raid. Many fires were caused, overwhelming the fire services. More than 500 lives were lost, with many historical buildings, including Coventry Cathedral, being razed to the ground.

Birmingham escaped a similar fate in a another raid about a week later. Its fire engines worked flat out to extinguish fires, coming close to running out of water and having to use Canal water. Two of our families were to experience enemy attacks near their homes that night. Bombs fell on Fenton Road, some houses away from Annie Barber's house, causing some injuries. That same night, Douglas Road, further up from where the Helms lived, was also attacked, causing injuries, but thankfully no deaths.

At 8.20 pm on 10 December 1940, St Mary The Virgin Church in Acocks Green was hit by a bomb, shortly after the confirmation class had gone to the cellar of the vicarage. The church roof was blown off. Stained-glass windows, one at the front of the church and one at the back, were shattered. The one at the back was blown to pieces too small to be recovered. However the Vicar, the Rev Philip Kelly, was able to save fragments of the front window, which was put together and put back in place when the church was fully restored after the war. Services had to be held at the Warwick Cinema (now a bowling alley) on the nearby Westley Road, until Easter 1941, by which time the church had been partially repaired.[11]

The church still bears some mementos of the air raid. The pulpit was originally on the left (as seen from the congregation), as it is in most English parish churches; its replacement is on the right. Also the destroyed stained-glass window was replaced by a plain glass one, leaving the church much more brightly lit as a consequence. There are still pockmarks in the wall near the votive candle stand on the left-hand side.

The following night one of the worst air raids on Birmingham took place.[12] A thirteen-hour raid, split into two phases, claimed 270 lives. The high death toll was partly the result of an

---

[11] *Acocks Green (1997)* by Michael Byrne, The History Press

[12] *The Luftwaffe Over Brum: Birmingham's Blitz From A Military Perspective*, by Steve Richards, also 'Birmingham Blitz: In their Own Words,' *Sunday Mercury* 5 Sep 2010.

RAF plan to attack German bombers with night fighters, with the anti-aircraft guns stood down and searchlights switched off to give the fighters a clear run. The fighters were converted Hampden bombers with limited firepower, and they did not succeed in shooting down any of the attackers. Towards the end of the night this plan was abandoned. The searchlights and guns went back into operation, destroying one bomber.

In the face of German air raids, acts of great bravery were carried out all over the country by members of the general public, police officers, fire fighters, and air raid wardens and service personnel. One local example was of George Inwood, a section commander with the Home Guard. On the night of 15/16 October 1940, he and his men were called by police to assist when bombs fell in the Five Ways area of the city. They discovered that several people were trapped in the cellar of a building, which had been hit by a bomb. As a result of damage caused by the bomb, the cellar was full of gas. George had himself lowered into the cellar with a rope. He went down twice, and pulled two unconscious people out to safety. Sadly, on a further attempt he was affected by the effects of the gas, and collapsed. He was pulled back up, but later died from the effects of inhaling the gas. He is buried in Yardley Cemetery just out-side Acocks Green.[13]

Another was that of William Mosedale, whose act of heroism took place on that dark night of 11/12 December 1940. A firefighter in Birming-ham for twenty-six years, he was on duty when a bomb destroyed the fire station in Sparkbrook where he worked, along with a house next door. Several of his colleagues were trapped in the rubble. He went back into the building repeat-ed, tunnelling through the rubble and adminis-tering oxygen to the survivors he found, and leading them to safety. In all, over a period of twelve hours his actions led to the rescue of twelve injured survivors, and the recovery of four bodies.

In response to the acts of great heroism in the face of the Blitz, the King had created a new medal, the George Cross, on 23 September 1940, stating:

'In order that [such people] should be worthily and promptly recognised, I have decided to create (...) a new mark of hon-our for men and women in all walks of civilian life, which will consist of the

---

13 *George Cross Heroes* (2003)by Michael Ashcroft, Headline Publishing.

George Cross, which will rank next to the Victoria Cross.'

Both Inwood and Mosedale were awarded the George Cross, the former posthumously. Their medals are on display at the Birmingham Art Gallery and Museum.

The raids were meant, in part, to break the spirit of the civilian population and cause panic and flight. In that they failed – the 'Blitz spirit' was seen in Birmingham as well as in other British cities. People took pride in continuing to live and work as normal – 'Business as usual' became a watchword.

Alec Priest was assigned to No. 5 Service Flying School, at RAF Ternhill in Shropshire, on 24 January 1941. He may well have been in aircrew training. He was to remain on that base, on a variety of assignments, until September of that year when he was transferred to RAF Aitcham, also in Shropshire.

ALEC(left) and LESLIE PRIEST
(Maureen Powell)

By the end of 1940, Gladys Barber was expecting a child. Her husband Basil enlisted in the RAF on 20 January 1941, at the recruitment centre at Cardington. The next day he was put on the reserve list, and released back into civilian life. He was called up at the end of February, reporting at the recruitment centre at Blackpool, part of Technical Training Command. A month later, on 28 March 1941, Gladys gave birth to their son, Gordon Anthony Barber ('Gordon Anthony').

At the start of April 1941, Basil was based closer to home. He had been assigned to No. 6 School of Technical Training, at RAF Hendesford in Staffordshire. This was a centre for RAF mechanics, and those from the Royal Navy's Fleet

Air Arm, to receive technical training on various airframes and engines.

On April 6 1941, Dennis was caught up in an escalation of the Greek conflict. Impatient with their Italian allies' stalemate in the campaign, German forces intervened, attacking Greece from the territory of Bulgaria. British, Australian and New Zealand soldiers arrived to support Greek forces on the ground, but Allied forces struggled against the invaders.

The squadron was soon to suffer heavy casualties. On Easter Sunday, 13 April 1941, six of the squadron's Blenheim bombers struck at German forces at Monastir Gap. On their way back they were attacked by German Bf 109 fighters, and all the British aircraft were shot down, with no survivors among the aircrews. The German advance continued relentlessly. N0. 211 Squadron fell back to its previous base at Tatoi, from where it returned to Egypt via Crete. All the British and Commonwealth forces were evacuated from mainland Greece in due course.

Meanwhile, Leslie Priest was on the Isle of Man. He had been transferred in early March 1941, to the No. 1 Defence Gunnery School, at RAF Ronaldsway. This was the island's peacetime airfield, commandeered for the war effort. Its purpose was to train airmen in gunnery to protect airfields from air attack.[14]. Personnel involved in the training were housed in Castletown, in boarding houses along the Promenade and houses within the town. At the Fort Island (Golf Links) Hotel, also commandeered, airmen were taught the mechanics and operation of Lewis, Browning and Bofors guns. They gained experience by firing at targets towed by aircraft. The training was a relatively short course, and Leslie was back at RAF Swinton Morley by April 10.

Also in early April 1941, Gordon Helm married Betsy May Allbut at St Mary the Virgin church. His father William was one of the witnesses. Betsy's address was given as Damson Lane in Elmdon Heath, Solihull, which was afterwards to appear in official documents as Gordon's new address.

The autumn brought another wedding. On September 29, Basil and Dennis's sister Valerie, remarried, to Stephen Field. He was a 'plater' and presumably exempt from conscription. Dennis was, of course, still serving abroad. Basil was

---

14 Isle of Man Government Website, https://www.gov-.im/categories/travel-traffic-and-motoring/isle-of-man-airport/about-isle-of-man-airport/history/1940-1945/no-1-gunnery-school/

not listed as a witness, so it is likely that he was not on leave and thus unable to attend.

Alf's ambulance unit was moved up and down the Western Desert, following the front. However, later in the year they were sent further east, to the then French territories of Syria and Lebanon. In so doing they were to take part in the aftermath of a little known campaign, in which Dennis Barber's squadron was also to feature.

ALF PRIEST
(Maureen Powell)

As we have already seen, the government of France, based at Vichy, had signed an armistice with Germany. Most French overseas territories were controlled by this government, although others had pledged loyalty to de Gaulle's Free French. In July 1940, controversially, the Royal Navy had attacked and sunk, or disabled most of the French fleet at 'Mers-el-Kebir' in Algeria – with heavy loss of French lives. This was due to a fear that it would fall into German hands, as the Vichy authorities had refused British requests to scuttle the ships, or to let them join the Allied cause.

Owing to German attempts to gain influence in the Middle East, the Allies decided to support the Free French in seizing the French colonies of Syria and Lebanon. Accordingly, Free French forces, backed by British, Australian, Indian, and other Allied forces, invaded Lebanon and Syria from Palestine on 8 June 1941.

Dennis's squadron were then based at RAF Aqir in Palestine, then a British mandated territory. The squadron's Blenheim bombers took part in bombing raids on Vichy French military and strategic targets. They remained based in Palestine, and never had cause to move into the contested territory.

The fighting continued for a little over a month, the Vichy authorities there surrendering on 12 July. The campaign was little reported, and is arguably not very well known in Britain even now. Apparently, British censorship limited reporting of the fighting as 'the French had to be seen only as a gallant ally under the heel of Nazi Germany the truth in Syria became the first casualty.'[15]

Alf's ambulance unit was attached to 14 Infantry Brigade, and they were sent eastwards to take part in the Syria-Lebanon campaign. On 7 July the brigade crossed the Sinai peninsula into Palestine by road and rail. Four days later, they crossed into Syria and made camp at Kissoué (Al-Kiswah) thirteen miles south of Damascus. While there, they received news that a truce had been arranged with the Vichy forces. The fighting was at an end, with a formal surrender from the Vichy French a few days later.

British service personnel were issued strict instructions not to mock the surrendered Vichy French soldiers. Their movement orders included the following instructions:

'Conduct towards Vichy Forces

Full honours of war have been been accorded to the Vichy Forces. They have never wanted to fight the British Empire and it is important from every aspect that good relations

---

15   *A B****rd of a Place: The Australians in Papua*, (2003) by Peter Brune Allen and Unwin.

should not be prejudiced...It is essential that in passing convoys there shall be no remarks or gestures to parties of Vichy Forces seen en route. Such action however well meant may be misconstrued. (…..) It is important to institute cordial relations between all ranks [of the two armies] as soon as possible. There is no limit placed on fraternisation therefore ordinary security measures of war continue. It is hoped that units will make every endeavour to arrange football matches etc as gear is available.'[16]

The ambulance unit remained in French territory for many weeks, being stationed for awhile at Zahle in Lebanon. In September they returned to Egypt by sea, and were almost immediately shipped onwards to the port of Tobruk in Libya, where Allied forces were then under siege by the German's and Italians. Alf's ambulance unit replaced an Australian one who had been rotated away earlier. Thankfully, the siege of Tobruk was lifted two months later, at the end of November.

Meanwhile, in June that year, a fateful event happened which was to have a great bearing on the outcome of the war. Germany attacked the Soviet Union on 22 July. German armoured divi-

---

[16] 173 Field Ambulance War Diary, National Archives WO 177/762

sions crossed the Soviet border, making swift progress and occupying all of Belarus and most of the Ukraine within a very short time. By September the Germans had laid siege to the Soviet Union's second city, Leningrad, now St Petersburg and by October they had reached the outskirts of the Soviet capital Moscow. The German advance stalled later with the onset of Winter, and this was the end of their rapid progress.

In August 1941, Leslie Priest was transferred to No. 12 Operational Training Unit (OTU), based at RAF Chipping Warden. As far as can be ascertained Leslie was not in aircrew training, his 'trade' in the RAF would have been airfield protection. The following month he was assigned to 2829 (Defence) Squadron. This may simply have been part of the organisation of the airfield defence trade leading to the creation of the RAF Regiment, which would include that Squadron, the following year. Leslie probably remained at Chipping Norton after being assigned to 2829 Squadron.

His relatives indicate that he probably became involved in an air crash over water, which may well have left him in the sea, possibly the North Sea, for some considerable time before being rescued; this is not mentioned in the limited available service records. Sadly, this experience was to take its toll on his health. In November he was admitted to the RAF hospital at Halton, where he was to remain until discharged almost a month later.

Many thousands of miles away in North Africa, Leslie's brother Alf was also unwell. Once again, the service records are not helpful. Alf's relatives believe that he was taken ill after drinking well water in the desert. They are of the view that the well had been poisoned by the enemy before their retreat - this is hard to establish so long after the event. The Unit War Diary maintained in Lebanon, records that men often did become ill through drinking well water, even when it was not poisoned. It would seem that Alf was evacuated on medical grounds, as his unit was still in the Western Desert when he was sent home. Probably in December, he started the long journey back home, again by ship around the Cape of Good Hope.

Also in late 1941, the last of our subjects joined the armed forces. Harry Helm joined the Portsmouth Division of the Royal Navy on 2 September 1941, as an Acting Able Seaman. He had been working at the Austin Motors until he was called up. Harry trained as a gunner on Defensively Equipped Merchant Ships (DEMS). As we have already seen, troopships and merchant ships travelled in convoys, with warships protecting the others from enemy attack. Defensive equipment enabled some of the merchant ships to protect themselves and others. The greatest danger was attack from submerged submarines, but DEMS equipment would not normally protect against these. Merchant ships were equipped with machine guns or light artillery to protect against enemy aircraft, and sometimes with heavier artillery to engage enemy surface warships, or submarines which surfaced to attack.

By December he was at *HMS President III,* an on-shore training establishment for DEMS gunners at Windsor and London. It is reported that at some time during his Naval career, he trained alongside a young officer called Prince Philip of Greece. The Prince, only a few months older than Harry, was later to marry the king's elder daughter, Princess Elizabeth and later became the long-lasting consort of the present Queen. [17]

---

[17] Wokingham Times, exact date unknown, April 2009, posted to Get Reading website 14 April 2011.

A DEMS GUN CREW DURING A PRACTICE DRILL
(Library and Archives of Canada)

December brought the long-anticipated women's call-up. Initially only women aged between twenty and thirty were conscripted. There were many exceptions, such as pregnant women or those with small children. Women were often sent to serve as forestry workers or farm hands, or to work in factories. Those who did join the military were assigned to non-combatant tasks.

Towards the end of the year, Basil's birthplace, West Bromwich, had its own decorated war heroine. Charity Bick had joined that town's Air Raid Precautions service the previous year, claiming to be sixteen - two years older than her actual age. She served as a cycle dispatch rider, serving with her father who was an air raid warden. During a heavy raid in late 1940, she helped her father put out fires caused by incendiary bombs, and was slightly injured falling through a charred roof. She also made many trips on her bicycle carrying essential messages, including three trips at the height of the raid. Her bravery was noted by the authorities, and recognised by the award of the George Medal. Charity received the medal from the King in September 1941, the youngest person to receive it to this day.[18]

18 IWM Website, http://www.iwm.org.uk/collections/ item/object/30006528.

Chapter Three: The End of the Beginning

December 1941 also saw a new front open in the war, one which would impact greatly on one of our subjects later on. On 7 December, Japanese aircraft and midget submarines attacked the US fleet at Pearl Harbor, Hawaii. Many American battleships and battle cruisers were damaged, or sunk, some of the latter to be re-floated and recovered in the following years. Crucially, American aircraft carriers were elsewhere and were not attacked. Within hours, Japanese forces invaded American and British territories in the Far East. This was a surprise attack, as Japan had not declared war. In the aftermath of the attack, Japan, Germany and Italy all declared war on the United States.

Hong Kong, the Philippines and Malaya all came under attack, and Guam was quickly overrun. Japanese aircraft bombed Singapore. On 10 December, the British battleship *Prince of Wales* and the battle-cruiser *Repulse* were both sunk off Malaya by Japanese dive bombers, with heavy loss of life. Britain continued to suffer reverses, as the colony of Hong Kong surrendered to Japanese forces on Christmas Day. In January 1942 the Japanese invaded the British territory of Burma (now Myanmar), which bordered British India.

Shortly before the New Year, Harry seems to have gone far towards qualifying as a DEMS gunner. He was stationed in London for a further week, and then at Liverpool for a few more days. On 11 January he embarked on the troopship *SS Orontes* for a voyage to Egypt. His service record refers to this trip as 'passage' so it seems he was a passenger rather than assigned as a DEMS gunner on the ship taking him there. *Orontes* was part of convoy WS 15, which left the Clyde on 11 January.

Less than a week into the voyage, Harry got a taste of the dangers of wartime life at sea. The convoy was attacked by a U-boat on 16 January while it was in the Bay of Biscay. Another troopship, the *Llangibby Castle*, was severely damaged by a torpedo and had to go to Portugal and later Gibraltar for repairs, having suffered twenty-six fatalities. For the other ships, the rest of the voyage seems to have gone on without incident. *Orontes* proceeded to Freetown, and continuing to Cape Town and Aden, after which those ships not heading further east travelled to the Suez Canal independently. Harry disembarked from *Orontes* on 8 March 1942, arriving at Port Said.

On 11 January, as Harry set sail for Egypt, Leslie Priest was discharged from the Air Force, apparently for health reasons. A week or so beforehand, Alf Priest had boarded the troopship *Arundel Castle* in South Africa. He seems to have changed ships on a voyage from the Suez Canal. The ship left Cape Town on 4 January, to reach Freetown on the 22nd of that month.

Sadly, Alf would not arrive there. On 17 January he passed away on board. The cause of death was recorded as 'interstitial nephritis', an inflammation of the kidneys. Whether this was caused by the same condition which led to his evacuation is not known. He was buried at sea, which was quite common then. Ships would have had little, or no facilities to preserve the remains of deceased people. The burial involved the body, wrapped up around a hammock, arranged on deck in the presence of part of the ship's company, and covered with a flag. After the reading of a special burial service, the body would be despatched over the side and into the sea. In military funerals, like Alf's, a party of soldiers or sailors would fire a volley of rifle shots over the body, as with a military funeral on land.

SAILORS FIRE A VOLLEY DURING A BURIAL AT SEA,
HMCS *PRINCE ROBERT*
(The Estate of John McKirdy Miller, from RCN History
website)

Following the Syrian campaign, Dennis Barber's 211 Squadron had been disbanded and its members withdrawn to Wadi Gazouza in Sudan in north-eastern Africa as part of a training unit. However, with the Japanese advance in the Far East, the Squadron was re-formed to be sent to reinforce British forces there. The squadron now included ground and aircrew from the Royal Australian Air Force. Dennis was promoted to Corporal on New Year's Day 1942.

On 17 January the bulk of the ground crew and equipment of No. 211 Squadron left by sea on the troopship *HMT Yoma* from Egypt, their aircraft having flown on ahead. The *Yoma* sailed to Aden, from where it joined a convoy heading for Colombo in Ceylon, now Sri Lanka. As they headed east, British and other allied territories fell to Japanese attacks. Malaya was occupied by 31 January, with British forces falling back onto Singapore. Following a siege of some two weeks, the latter territory surrendered on 15 February, with 85,000 British and Empire service personnel falling into Japanese captivity. Widespread atrocities were carried out by Japanese forces against captured Allied prisoners in all the occupied areas, including the massacre of Allied patients and medical staff at the British Military Hospital in Singapore.

A trend was emerging. Allied reinforcements were arriving too late to be of much use, and were landing in areas about to fall to the Japanese. Hence ,many of them walked almost straight from their troopships into the prisoner-of-war camps.

The *Yoma* landed at Oosthaven, now Bandar Lampung, in Sumatra on 14 February 1942. This was part of the Dutch East Indies, now Indonesia. From there it proceeded to Batavia aka Jakarta on Java, where the ground crew, including Dennis, disembarked. The squadron aircrafts had initially been based at existing RAF bases in Malaya before they fell. Missions had already been flown against the Japanese, but with little success as the latter were beginning to achieve air supremacy. By the time the *Yoma* arrived, the aircraft were based at Kalidjati on Java, having briefly been at Palembang on Sumatra.

By now Japanese forces had landed elsewhere in the Dutch East Indies, landing at Sumatra on 14 February. No. 211 Squadron was based on Java, and invasion was known to be imminent. Hard decisions had to be taken as to whether to commit to a battle in defence of the island, or to evacuate what could be saved of the squadron's personnel and equipment. No missions were flown after 22 February.

On the night of 27 February, a Japanese fleet defeated a joint British, Australian, American and Dutch naval force in the Battle of Java Sea. It was a major naval defeat for the Allies, as they lost five ships and more than two thousand sailors, while the Japanese suffered one destroyer damaged and less than forty dead. This put an end to any Allied hopes of intercepting a Japanese invasion force. The following day, Japanese troops landed in Java.

The Japanese moved swiftly to crush all resistance. British, Dutch and Australian forces fought back unsuccessfully. Kalidjati airfield was attacked by the Japanese ground forces on 1 March. Dutch troops and British airmen fought back but were overrun. Some escaped by road to Bandung but the rest were captured. It is reported that many of the prisoners taken then were killed by the Japanese shortly afterwards.[19]

The British had by then realised that there would be little chance of escape. On 26 February, the Prime Minister, Mr. Winston Churchill, had sent the following telegram to the British commander on Java, Air Vice Marshall Maltby:

> 'I send you and all ranks of the British Forces who have stayed behind in Java my best wishes for success and honour in the great fight that confronts you. Every day gained is precious. And I know that you will do everything humanly possible to prolong the battle. Ends.'[20]

Some British forces sought to withdraw. On 2 March a ship, the *Tung Song*, arrived to collect some RAF ground crew, but inevitably there was not enough space for everyone. A Wing Commander Gregson was one of the senior officers

---

[19] *Prisoners in Java* (a book of published accounts of Java FEPOW survivors, henceforth *PIJ*) p. 71, Jim Ralphs et al.

[20] *PIJ* p 78, George Michaelis.

who supervised the evacuation, and at the last moment he declared that he himself would not be evacuated but would stay with the men [21]. Likewise, it is said that around the same time, one hundred and fifty officers and men from Dennis's squadron boarded the ship *Orcades*, which was about to leave Java for Australia. However, when asked to volunteer to give up their places to accommodate Dutch women and children still ashore, every one of the men gave up his place. The officers and airmen went ashore again to await their fate.[22] Air Vice Marshall Maltby himself was not evacuated, and was to spend the rest of the war as a prisoner of the Japanese.

A little under a week later the Dutch command on Java surrendered. British service personnel still there were informed of this by their superiors, and told that they were now prisoners and not to fire on any Japanese forces that they may encounter. In the event it was to be several days before many British service personnel would actually see their Japanese captors. Dennis's own date of capture as provided by Java

[21] *PIJ* p. 56, Tom Coles.

[22] 211 Squadron website, LW Abbs. http://www.211squadron.org/lw_abbs.html

FEPOW Association is given as 8 March 1942, which is the date of the actual Dutch surrender.

At the time no confirmation was received by the British authorities that Dennis had been captured alive. By now accounts of atrocities against British and other Allied prisoners had become public knowledge in the UK. Dennis's family, therefore, would only have known that he was missing. They may well have feared that he had been killed, either during the fighting, or shortly after capture.

Back in England, meanwhile, the Priest family would have been dealing with Leslie's illness as well as the sad news of Alf's passing. It is not noted whether Alec was given any sort of compassionate leave in respect of either event. His record shows that later in January 1942 he was assigned to No. 12 School of Technical Training at RAF Melksham in Wiltshire, where instrument makers and armourers were trained on ground airframes rather than on flying aircraft. On the other hand, Eric's records show that he was granted some compassionate leave in February 1942, presumably linked to his family's recent upheavals.

As we have seen, Gordon Helm's colleagues in the Royal Army Pay Corps were working and living in Leicester town centre. As they and their surroundings were at risk from air raids, they took part in the struggle against the potential attacks – they took part in 'fire-watching,' looking out from rooftops to alert others of any potential air attacks, and also putting out incendiary devices, firebombs, that might fall.

In March 1942 Defence Minister Mr. Duncan Sandys said in response to a parliamentary question:

> 'In order to have available in the centre of the city a reserve of men to assist in the event of an air raid, about 400 members of the Royal Army Pay Corps stationed at Leicester are required to sleep at the Pay Offices one week in every four. These men are relieved of all other guard duties and fatigues.' [23]

Responding to an MP's question, the Minister denied that the men were doing as many as 154 hours of fire-watching per month, and that their hours exceeded those of civilians performing that same duty.

Meanwhile, Basil Barber's trade path in the RAF was about to change. He had not completed training as a mechanic, but was now to transfer to aircrew on bombers. All aircrew were volunteers, so Basil would have put himself forward for this. Air raids on the UK had declined in numbers and Birmingham itself was to suffer its last major raid in July

---

[23]   Hansard HC Deb 1013/72 Vol 378 cols 914-5.

of that year. However, as German air attacks on Britain declined, the RAF was stepping up its attacks on Germany and occupied Europe. As early as September 1940, Churchill had recognised the importance of bomber aircraft to the war effort, writing in a directive that 'the fighters are our salvation but the bombers alone provide the means of victory.'[24]

Britain had started the war with a small force of light and medium bombers. These would attack in relatively small formations and would try to hit precise targets, such as a factory or a dockyard. However, by 1942 it was clear that this tactic would have limited success, as bombs often went astray due to direction-finding and bomb-aiming technology not being well developed. In 1941, the government's Butt Report, based on analysis of bomb-damage photographs taken by spy planes, indicated that most raids were going wide of the mark.[25]

With this in mind, a new tactic was adopted by the British government. It was known as 'area bombing,' it is commonly called 'carpet bombing.' In brief, rather than a small number of bombers attempting to hit a relatively small target, a very large force

[24] *Churchill's War Lab: Code Breakers, Boffins, and Innovators: The Mavericks Churchill Led to Victory* (2011) by Taylor Downing, Abacus.

[25] Ibid.

would seek to destroy the area containing it. Often the bomber force would number as many as a thousand, and the area sought to be destroyed would be a whole town or a neighbourhood of a city, containing the relevant target. The new policy adopted by the government anticipated that the workers would be demoralised by the destruction of their houses, and the risk of death in air raids, and that this would affect enemy morale.[26] Weeks after this became government policy, Air Vice Marshall Arthur Harris, soon to be knighted, became the commander in chief of Bomber Command. He would pursue the new policy vigorously.

This would cause massive devastation, and often thousands of deaths on the ground, mostly civilian. Harris cared little about high German civilian casualties – in his view, 'the Nazis' had brought it on themselves by bombing civilian populations in Warsaw, Rotterdam and in England. As he said, they had 'sown the wind, and would reap the whirlwind.'[27]

However, as there would be many bombers in the air, there would also be heavy casualties among the aircrew. Enemy fighter aircraft and anti-aircraft guns would have no

---

[26] Air Ministry Directive to the RAF (S.46368/111 DCAS) 14 February 1942, and also Lord Cherwell's 'dehousing' memorandum to Churchill, 30 March 1942).

[27] *Bombing Germany: The Final Phase* by Tim Redding, and also Hosea 8:7.

shortage of targets to fire at, all in a lengthy, spread-out formation, the 'bomber stream'. It was the heavy losses caused to aircrew by this strategy, rather than the civilian casualties which resulted, which led to Harris being dubbed 'Butcher' by RAF aircrew. The press called him 'Bomber', and he is better known by that nickname of 'Bomber Harris.'

The new tactic needed the RAF to vastly increase its bomber force, and also to develop larger aircraft, which would carry a heavier weapon load. The small, two-engined bombers with which the RAF started the war, such as the Wellington and the Hampden, would be replaced by Stirling, Halifax and Lancaster bombers, each with four engines.

These aircraft were more complex than their predecessors. It was decided that rather than carry two pilots as before, they would carry one pilot and an airman, or officer fulfilling the new role of 'flight engineer,' in addition to the navigator, wireless operator and gunners that bombers had always carried. The engineer's task would be to monitor the instruments, and do various mechanical tasks on the plane. It was this role that Basil Barber started working towards in the spring of 1942.

A former flight engineer said of his duties:

'My job was everything mechanical on the aircraft. I would start the engines, and during take-off I would control the throttles once the pilot needed to put hands on the control column. I had to get the wheels

73

up and trim the flaps, and during the flight I kept an eye on all the instruments. It was almost a co-pilot's job, but there was only one control column. I was sufficiently trained that I could fly the aircraft.' [28]

FLIGHT ENGINEER IN A LANCASTER
BOMBER
(IWM [public domain])

28 Edgar Childs DFC, quoted in 'Why The Forgotten heroes of Bomber Command Deserve A Memorial,' *Daily Telegraph*, 24 October 2008.

Basil started training as a flight engineer at No 11 Recruits' Centre, Skegness on 15 April 1942. He would have been with a mixture of other experienced airmen who had already trained as ground mechanics, and new recruits who had entered the service with a view to becoming flight engineers.

The expansion of the bomber force involved large numbers of aircrew from overseas. Many men from all over the British Empire – from India, Jamaica, Sierra Leone and other countries – came to Britain to serve as aircrew. The RAF also had 'exile' squadrons made up of pilots from Poland, Norway and other occupied nations. In addition, the governments of Australia, Canada and New Zealand had signed an agreement by which units of their own air forces would be attached to the RAF. These were known as 'Article Fifteen' squadrons after the clause in the agreement between the nations which allowed for such attachments. The squadrons all had numbers starting with '4'. However, high casualty rates meant that replacement crew members often did not come from the relevant nation, so the Article Fifteen squadrons always contained a large number of British airmen and officers, and many from other countries.

Meanwhile, Alec Priest, continued with his training. In mid-1942, he went to two other schools of technical training in rapid succession. First was No. 11 Technical Trainign School (TTS) at Hereford, which provided conversion courses for electricians, instrument makers and armourers. Afterwards, in May, he was sent to No. 10 TTS, at Kirkham in Lancashire, where flight mechanics and riggers were trained on 'instructional airframes' – effectively, training on dummy aircraft.

The summer was to bring another significant development for the Priest family. Eric went off to war again. Like his late brother, he was assigned to British forces in the North African campaign. Eric was also to be a driver, in his case attached to 5 Mobile Ambulance Company.

ERIC PRIEST
(Maureen Powell)

He embarked at Greenock in Scotland, on 29 May 1942, with convoy WS19P. He probably travelled with almost three thousand other troops on the Dutch merchant ship *SS Christiaan Huygens*. The convoy took the long route around the Cape of Good Hope, stopping in the huge natural harbour at Freetown on 15 June 1942, and leaving there four days later. After stops at Cape Town and Durban in early July, the ships dispersed at Aden and arrived independently at

Suez, on 23 July 1942. The convoy seems to have had a safe journey with no attacks.

Eric was attached to different units at various locations along the Western Desert as the campaign continued. This was a crucial time for the Allies' war effort. Rommel's *Afrika Korps* was having considerable success against the British Eighth Army. Some weeks before Eric's arrival in Egypt, the German and Italian forces had captured the port of Tobruk in Libya. Eighty thousand Allied troops, mostly British and South African, surrendered - the second largest number of British and Empire forces captured, after the fall of Singapore earlier in the year. This occurred shortly after the Axis forces decisively defeated the Allied forces at the Battle of Gazala.

The Eighth Army commander, General Claude Auchinlek, ordered a retreat deeper into Egypt, closer to his base. The approach of the Axis forces apparently caused a panic in the Egyptian port of Alexandria (a main Royal Navy base), with local businesses putting up Italian or German flags to show loyalty to the expected new masters. [29].There was also widespread looting, and a lot of naval stores were destroyed to pre-

---

[29] David Hume, *Life and Times of James Hume*, by David Hume, containing James' wartime memoir http://www.alawrencefamily.net,

vent them falling into enemy hands. However, even as Eric arrived in Egypt, Auchinlek's forces were fighting their Axis counterparts to a stalemate at the first battle of El Alamein, which halted the Axis advance towards Alexandria.

About a month later, Prime Minister Churchill removed Auchinlek as Eighth Army commander. He was replaced by General William Gott, who was killed shortly afterwards when his aeroplane was shot down by German aircraft.   The new commander appointed was General Bernard Montgomery ('Monty'), whose appointment was to have a great effect on the desert campaign and the rest of the war.

Eric seems to have undergone further training and acquired some extra skill, such that on 19 September 1942 he was granted SPP ('Special Proficiency Pay') for his additional abilities. It seems he remained with a mobile ambulance company for the next few months. He would have still been with them during the decisive Second Battle of El Alamein in late October/early November 1942 in which Montgomery's Eighth Army defeated the Axis forces and sent them retreating westwards, a battle which Prime Minister Churchill referred to as 'the end of the beginning.'

Later in November 1942, another crucial development occurred in the North African campaign. British and American forces landed in the French North African territories, which were controlled by the Vichy regime. After brief resistance, these territories surrendered to the Allies. Axis forces had moved into French Tunisia by this time, however. Overall, the Italian and German forces were now facing Allied forces on either side.

As a consequence of this campaign, Germany occupied the Vichy-controlled zone of France. The French navy there scuttled its ships based at Toulon so that the Germans could not take them over.

Meanwhile, far away in Asia, Dennis was in Japanese captivity along with thousands of other Allied prisoners of war. Along with many of his 211 Squadron comrades, he was initially held on the island of Java.

Allied prisoners of the Japanese were subject to a harsh regime. Most other countries had signed and ratified the Geneva Conventions, which laid down guaranteed minimum standards for treatment of prisoners of war. Japan, however, had signed the Convention but not brought it into force. As a result ,it did not consider itself bound by its provisions.

Allied prisoners were made to shave their heads as Japanese soldiers did. They had to bow to any Japanese soldier, irrespective of the latter's rank. Prisoners of war held by other countries considered themselves as having a duty to escape. However, the Japanese ordered their captives to sign promises not to escape. Breach of such an agreement would lead to the prisoners being executed, usually by firing squad, or being beheaded.

The prisoners were forced to do hard physical labour, with no distinction made between officers and enlisted men in this regard. Their health often deteriorated. Camps would have small clinics but they had very little by way of medicines, so the mortality rate was high. The prisoners' situation was sadly to get even worse in the following months and years.

Physical violence towards prisoners by their Japanese guards was common. Arguably, this reflected the fact that such violence was common by Japanese officers and non-commissioned officers towards their own subordinates. Bill Marshall,[30] writes of the Japanese, 'They appeared to treat their own people as they treated us. The officers beat the NCOs, who beat the ordinary soldiers, who beat us. We were at the tail end of it all.'

---

[30] Bill Marshall, Java FEPOW journal, Jan 2017.

One particularly sadistic guard was a Sergeant-Major Masao Mori, who was notorious for giving prisoners severe beatings with his ever-present bamboo cane. He spoke next to no English and would be accompanied by his interpreter, a Korean soldier called Kasiyama. The latter was believed to sometimes misinterpret remarks from the prisoners to fire up Mori and make his behaviour even more violent.[31] The two were known as 'Blood' and 'Slime' respectively, after the symptoms of the dreaded disease amoebic dysentery.

Mori – who we shall meet later - was to achieve lasting fame, or rather infamy. A fellow prisoner-of-war in the camps, the British author Laurens van der Post, included a character, Sergeant-Major Hara, based on Mori in the story collection - *The Seed And The Sower*, later filmed as *Merry Christmas, Mr Lawrence*.

The various camps in Java held prisoners from many different countries, many of them Australian, British or Dutch. In the early months, this worked to the prisoner's advantage as the Dutch, many of whom had lived locally before the war, would make contact with the local Javanese people. At that stage the prisoners were

---

[31] Tony Cowling, 'My Life With the Samurai: A POW In Indonesia' p.92.

allowed to barter with the local people for food to supplement the meagre camp diet.

Back in the UK, Alec Priest's service career came to an end later that year. He was discharged from the Royal Air Force under a provision of the King's Regulations 1942, as not reaching the standard of physical fitness required. This left Eric as the last Priest brother in the armed forces proper. Frederick Junior was still serving part-time with the Home Guard.

The New Year saw a new arrival for one of our subjects. A boy was born to Gordon Helm and his wife in late January. Gordon appears on the birth certificate as informant, so he must happily have been on home leave when the birth was registered four days later. He is recorded as being a Sergeant in the Pay Corps.

Sadly, in February 1943, Leslie's condition deteriorated. By then he was at the City Sanatorium, Yardley Green Road, suffering from tuberculosis. He passed away on 14 February, aged only twenty. Although already discharged, he was still apparently on the books of the Air Force such that he is commemorated on the War Graves Commission website. Alec was named on the death certificate as the informant. Four days after his death, Leslie was buried at St Mary the Virgin Church, and his burial place now bears a War Graves Commission gravestone.

Harry Helm had been on attachment to a shore establishment, Post Said, in Egypt. On 12 September 1942 his training ended and he was confirmed as an Able Seaman. In the new year, he was finally assigned to a ship, *SS Dafila*, on 11 January 1943, although he does not seem to have boarded her until some weeks later. The ship was of 1940 tons, and had a crew of about sixty all told, including gunners. *Dafila* was described as an Armament Stores and Issuing Ship, and her task was to go up and down the coast providing arms and ammunition to the fleet. At that stage it was armed with three guns, two .5 'pom pom' guns, and a heavier 12 pound gun [32]

In February, the *Dafila* was assigned to even more hazardous duties. It landed all its naval ammunition and was converted to transport large quantities of case fuel as well as ammunition, to the Eighth Army. Loading commenced in mid- February and finished on the 27th. Another small ship, the *Kaying*, was assigned to the same task, and loaded up accordingly with petrol and ammunition. Apparently the idea was that one ship was likely to be sunk, so if this happened the other one would get through with its precious cargo.

---

[32] Hume, op cit. Note 28. James Hume was an officer on the *Dafila*.

Dafila had been fitted with more weapons. Two 20mm Oerlikon anti-aircraft guns had been added to the wings of the bridge. Harry embarked with seven other gunners, a mixture of soldiers and sailors, apparently replacing a previous team of Royal Marines. Other than the gunners, the crew now totalled twenty-nine. Presumably there were far less crewmen than usual because of the nature of the trip and the considerable cargo. The voyage was considered to be so hazardous that the crew were ordered to leave all their valuables, and personal effects ashore.

On 1 March, *Dafila* and *Kaying* left Alexandria harbour and assembled with the rest of their convoy. Six destroyers were to escort five merchant ships, an indication of the importance of the cargo.

An engine fault left *Dafila* stranded behind the rest of the convoy, on the following day. One destroyer remained with it, while engineers struggled to repair the engine. At 1600 hours, six German Stuka dive bombers attacked the ship. A bomb exploded nearby, damaging the steering gear. However, the guns on *Dafila* and the escort fired at the enemy aircraft, driving them off. The engine fault was repaired shortly afterwards, but as it was now dark it was decided that the damaged steering gear would be repaired the following day, with the ship now sailing in circles to keep up with its escort.

The following morning the steering gear was repaired and *Dafila* and her escort continued to sail westward. However at 1300, as the crew were having lunch, the ship came under attack – once again by six German Stuka dive bombers. The attackers were driven off by gunfire, despite some bombs falling close to the ships.

There were no more attacks, and *Dafila* reached Tobruk harbour at 1:00 hours the next morning. After a few days spent there, it left with the rest of the convoy, for Tripoli. There were some air and submarine attacks on the way but no loss or damage was caused.

At Tripoli, the petrol and ammunition was taken off *Dafila* and *Kaying*. They had beaten the odds, and both arrived safely. The ships stayed in Tripoli harbour while they and other ships were being unloaded. While there the harbour itself, and some of the other ships, came under attack by German Ju-88 bombers and by Italian frogmen seeking to plant limpet mines. The harbour itself and many other ships suffered significant damage, not affecting either *Dafila* nor *Kaying*.

Early on the morning of 19 March, *Dafila*, *Kaying* and other ships set off in convoy on the return journey to Alexandria. They were now carrying only empty barrels as ballast, and only had a light escort of destroyers.

Some hours later, after daybreak, *Dafila's* luck ran out. At 8:34, a German U-Boat, U-593, struck *Dafila* with two torpedoes. The U-Boat then shifted its attention to the *Kaying*, torpedoing it as well.

As both ships had been loaded with petrol until recently, both would have been affected by fumes. *Dafila* exploded and sank almost at once, many on board being thrown clear of the wreckage. *Kaying*, seriously damaged, managed to stay afloat. It was to sink the next day, in heavy seas.

Of the thirty-seven men on board *Dafila*, twenty-two were killed and fifteen survived. Three of the dead were gunners, as were five of the survivors including Harry. Of the dead gunners, two were soldiers and the other was a Royal Navy sailor. Harry and some of the other survivors were rescued from the sea by a South African warship, after spending many hours in the water. By comparison, *Kaying* lost seven crew members and two gunners, with sixty-seven crew members and four gunners being rescued. [33]

Harry was then transported to Alexandria, the trip lasting two days. Some survivors were landed at Cerna in eastern Libya and then taken to Alexandria by land - it may be that Harry took this route too. He is recorded as having been at *HMS Canopus*, a naval shore base at Alexandria, for the following eight days, probably admitted to a sick bay. He then spent the month of April at two different DEMS bases, Port Said and Port Tewfik, before going to sea again in early May.

Also in March, the International Red Cross Committee informed the British authorities that Dennis Barber was alive and a prisoner. The information would have been passed on to Dennis's family. No doubt they would have been happy to know that he was still alive, but apprehensive as to his well-being, with good reason.

Men of 211 Squadron, with other prisoners of the Japanese, were marshalled at Jaarmarkt

---

[33] The fortunes of war: U-593, still operating in the Mediterranean Sea, was successfully attacked by two Allied destroyers at the end of the year, and sunk. While most submarines sunk in the war were lost either with all hands or with heavy loss, the entire crew of U-593 were captured alive. Uboat.net website, https://**uboat**.net/**boats/u593**.htm.

Camp on Java in April. It was clear that they were destined for some new work allocation. The Japanese mockingly referred to the prisoners as 'Churchill's thank-you men,' a free labour force gifted to them by the British [34]. Maybe the Japanese had heard of the Prime Minister's 'stay behind' telegram.

At Jaarmarkt, the 211 Squadron and other prisoners were first shown a film – a propaganda movie praising the Pearl Harbor attack. They were then addressed by a Japanese officer, Colonel Anami, who had a long beard and whom the British nicknamed 'Whiskers.' He announced that the prisoners would be going to 'a holiday camp where the food will be very good and the work not too strenuous.' This was to prove inaccurate.

The prisoners were to build a new airstrip on Haruku, one of the 'Spice Islands' near Java. The prisoners were not told that Japan had suffered serious reverses over the past year, including a major sea defeat by the Americans at Midway and one on land by the hands of Australian forces at Milne Bay, Papua New Guinea. The Japanese wanted to have more airfields to help repel the Allied resurgence. Japan had lost four aircraft carriers at Midway, and so the idea

---

[34] *My Life With The Samurai* by Anthony Cowling, pp 69-70.

arose of making islands like Haruku into 'unsinkable aircraft carriers.'

The prisoners detailed to work at this new camp, learned swiftly that the sadistic Mori was to be going with them. They saw him viciously beat their commanding officer, Squadron Leader Pitts, on the parade ground. Disconcerting though this was, they also had to cope with the circumstances of their travel.

The first set of prisoners making up the initial draft to that island, travelled on the ship *Amagi Maru*. There were about a thousand prisoners on that ship, a 3,700 troop transport. Another thousand prisoners made up that draft, some carried on the *Kinitana Maru*.

Conditions on the voyage were severe – the Japanese prisoner-of-war transports were called 'hell ships.' The prisoners were packed into the depths of the ships like sardines. A newspaper article containing a survivor's account of the conditions on board the *Amagi Maru* stated, 'With no space to move and in complete darkness, it resembled the ships used to transport slaves from Africa centuries before.'[35] The voyage was hair-raising even before it started as armaments were loaded aboard the transport ships as well as people. Another transport ship

---

[35] Bob Morrill, *Brighton and Hove Argus* 24.11.15.

exploded while being loaded – as it happened, there were no prisoners on that ship but this still struck terror into the hearts of the captives on the other ships.

The prisoners suffered in the holds with limited food and water. They could only use latrines when they were allowed up to the deck where the facilities were located. To make it worse, the voyage lasted a lot longer than it need have. Another survivor recollects that the trip should have taken three to four days, but it took nineteen.[36]

The ships stopped over in Ambon, where the prisoners helped offload bombs and barrels of aviation fuel. Afterwards they finally arrived at Haruku, on 4 May 1943. Unlike Ambon, the much smaller island of Haruku did not have a modern port, and the prisoners had to be transported by small locally-made boats, known as sampans, in several trips.

The camp on the island had basic facilities. There were a few half-constructed bamboo huts, some with roofs. There were no latrines, and just a stream for drinking water. The two thousand men or so who had left Java relatively

---

[36] BBC Wales Blog, account of David Arthur Harries, 11 November 2011. www.bbc.co.uk/blogs/wales/entries/188fb5cc116-3bd1-a244-2744df31e68a

fit and well were now weakened by the voyage, and some were suffering from amoebic dysentery. The rainy season was just starting, and so conditions were to get worse over the following days.

The men's task was to level the hills on the island and build an airstrip. This involved hard work involving breaking rocks and lumps of coral. However, within a few days of their arrival, dysentery broke out in the camp. Soon twenty or thirty men were being buried in a day.[37] Such men as remained fairly healthy were expected to continue with the work. It was difficult to raise the required working party of two hundred and fifty men.[38]

Squadron Leader Pitts, the British prisoners' commanding officer, advised the camp commandant that the building of a latrine over the sea would make conditions better – it would transfer excrement away from the ditches and make the island more habitable. The commandant, Captain Kurashima, apparently opposed this as the sea was considered the property of the

37 PIJ, *Prisoners in Java* p. 182, Fred Freeman.

38 PIJ, p. 183, Robert Hoynes.

Japanese Emperor, who was seen by his people as virtually divine. [39]

At length, the building of the latrine over the sea was authorised, on the basis that if it was not built, the prisoners would die at a faster rate and the work on the airstrip would not be done. By some accounts, Sergeant Major Mori, who held real power on the island, gave the order for the building of the latrine.[40] Work on the airstrip was temporarily halted while the latrine was constructed. By all accounts the death rate decreased considerably after it was built.

One of the prisoners, the British airman and botanist Leslie Audus, had the idea of growing yeast using rice husks. The yeast was then mixed with the prisoners' meagre rations to add Vitamin B to their diet. This improved their general health and increased their chances of survival. Mori could have stopped this, but he did not do so – by some accounts, he was bribed with alcoholic 'hooch' brewed from the yeast! [41]

---

[39] *My Life With The Samurai* by Anthony Cowling (1996), Kangaroo Press p.97.

[40] *PIJ*, p.201, Don Peacock.

[41] *PIJ*, p. 211-2, Joe Fitzgerald.

While Dennis and his fellow prisoners toiled and suffered on the ground on Haruku, his brother Basil was taking to the air thousands of miles away. On 23 February 1943, he had been assigned to 306 Ferry Training Unit at RAF Templeton in Wales, where aircrews trained on Beaufort light bombers. Months later, on 27 July, he was assigned to Coastal Command's 304 Ferry Training Unit, based at Port Ellen in Scotland, which flew Beaufighter fighter bombers.

The persecution of Jewish people in Germany and occupied Europe was well-known. However, from 1942 onwards, it took a different step which was largely kept secret. Jewish people were rounded up and 'deported' towards camps in the eastern parts of Germany, or in occupied Poland. Officially they were being 'resettled.' In fact they were being worked to death, or simply murdered. Other categories of people deemed undesirable by the Nazis, such as gay people and Roma Gypsies, were also sent to these camps.

Chapter Four: Towards A Second Front

Meanwhile, bitter fighting continued on the Eastern Front. Another winter was wreaking havoc on the German forces. A large German and Romanian army had been surrounded by Soviet forces, at Stalingrad on the Volga river. After a prolonged siege, lasting from August 1942 and ending in February 1943, the Germans and Romanians surrendered. This was a turning point in the war in the East. The Soviets pressed for a 'Second Front' – a landing by the Western Allies on the European mainland - so that the task of fighting the Germans on the ground in Europe would be shared.

Accordingly, many soldiers in Britain prepared for the possibility of being posted overseas on combat duties. Even those whose normal tasks would be overwhelmingly behind the lines, went through weapons training in case they might be caught up in an ambush, or have to defend a base from being overrun. In the summer of 1943, Gordon Helm did his infantry weapons course at the Northern Command Weapons Training School, at the Army Barracks at Catterick, Yorkshire. He started the course on 5 May and completed it about three weeks later, passing with flying colours.

Harry had remained ashore for some time following the sinking of the *Dafila*. His records show that his next two postings were with DEMS gunners in Port Said and Port Tewfik in Egypt, presumably as a standby to be assigned to any ship needing replacement, or additional gunners. In May 1943, he boarded the merchant ship *SS Ocean Pride*. He would spend the next few months with that ship, sailing to Alexandria, Tripoli, and back to Port Said. His Service record indicates that the ship was attacked by enemy aircraft on 10 July. The ship's records do not mention any damage or casualties, so it would seem that the attack was driven off without any further incident.

The records do not make it clear what cargo the *Pride* carried. By then the North Africa campaign was coming to an end, as the *Afrika Korps* surrendered on 13 May 1943. Rommel had been flown out beforehand.

There were lots of Allied troop movements in North Africa, as the first part of the Second Front was going to be launched from there. On 10 July 1943, Allied forces including American, British, and Canadian soldiers, attacking from North Africa, landed on the island of Sicily just off the southern tip of Italy. After over a month of hard fighting, the Allies secured the island and the Axis survivors were evacuated to the Italian mainland.

On Harry's return to Egypt in July 1943, he once again went to serve at shore establishments. First he was assigned to DEMS at Port Said, *HMS Sphinx,* an accommodation camp and then DEMS Alexandria. He stayed there until 18 August 1943, when he was assigned to the *Christiaan Huygens*, which left for Scotland as part of Convoy MKF 22. Thus he returned to the UK on the ship which may have carried Eric Priest to Africa the previous year. The voyage home seems to have passed without incident, the ships arriving on the Clyde in Scotland about a month later.

MV *CHRISTIAAN HUYGENS*
(Tropen Museum, part of the National
Museum of World Cultures)

Basil Barber was back on the ground for the next few stages of his training. Much of this was at the School of Technical Training at Glamorgan. However, for one week in October he was back in Birmingham, attached to the Austin Motor Company. This establishment had made cars before the war, and would do so afterwards. However in wartime its tasks included making combat aircraft. Basil's attachment would seem to have been with a view to assisting him to understand the workings of the heavy bombers. He was probably attached not to the Austin factory at Longbridge that made Rover cars until fairly recently and where some MG cars are still assembled, but to the 'shadow factory' at nearby Cofton Hackett where various combat aircraft, including the four-engined Short Stirling bomber, were made. He may also have spent time at RAF Elmdon, the peacetime Elmdon Airport that became Birmingham Airport, where some of the bombers were flight-tested. The attachment was brief, but presumably Basil would have taken the opportunity to visit his wife and young son. The following month, he was promoted to the rank of Sergeant, a necessary step to serving as aircrew.

Harry Helm, meanwhile, had spent several months at various shore establishments. These included being stationed with DEMS gunners at Glasgow and the Clyde. However, he was also at *HMS Safeguard* for a little over three weeks. This was a converted country house, commandeered by the Navy and used for rest and recuperation of DEMS gunners, especially those recuperating from injury, or shock.[42]

After a short spell again assigned to his old training base of *HMS President III*, Harry was back on his way north to Scotland. He was based briefly at DEMS Glasgow, and then was assigned to a seagoing vessel for the first time in months. The ship was SS *Ocean Messenger*, and Harry was assigned to it effective 2 December 1943.

The ship, with others, left Loch Ewe later that month as part of the convoy JW55B, heading for the Soviet Arctic ports. They were to play a role in a major naval engagement, the Battle of North Cape. These were part of a vital supply line transporting weapons and other supplies from the Western Allies to assist the Soviets in keeping up the fight against Nazi Germany and her allies.

The Arctic convoys were among the most arduous for the Merchant and Royal Navies. Merchant ships, escorted by warships, would sail from Scotland, or Iceland, around the very top of Norway and then onto the Soviet Arctic ports of Murmansk or Archangel. The return trip would sometimes involve the ships carrying Soviet goods in repayment, sometimes timber, or

[42] BBC website 'WW2: People's War' Ivy Garraway, submitted 23 November 2005.

gold.[43] The sailors had to contend with the freezing temperatures as well as the enemy forces. They faced what one historian called the 'triple whammy' of German submarines, surface raiders, and bombers. The crushing Arctic ice would sometimes drive convoy ships closer to the Norwegian coast and, thus, closer to the German bomber bases there. The combination of extreme weather and heavy enemy attacks led to the Prime Minister calling these voyages 'the worst journey in the world.'

As the war turned against the Germans on the Eastern Front, the German Navy decided to take drastic steps to destroy, or scatter Soviet-bound convoys and disrupt the flow of supplies to the Soviet Union. The Germans decided to deploy one of their surviving large surface ships, the battleship *Scharnhorst*.

The ships of this convoy were effectively used as a decoy, to lure the *Scharnhorst* from her base in Norway to her destruction – along with a returning convoy, RA 55A. In addition to the normal destroyer escorts, the convoys were also shadowed by Royal Navy units known as Force 1 and Force 2, each consisting of many larger warships, including the battleship *Duke of York*, as well as the cruisers *Belfast, Norfolk,*

---

43 *The Battle of the Atlantic*, (2015) by Jonathan Dimbleby, Penguin.

Sheffield and *Jamaica*. Force 1 also included a ship of the exiled Norwegian navy, the *Strood*.

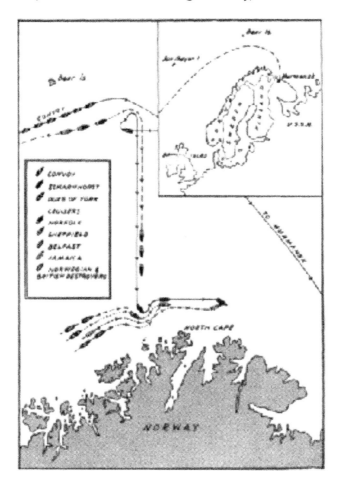

The BATTLE OF THE NORTH CAPE
(US Navy 'All Hands' magazine[public domain])

Scharnhorst and five destroyers left the port of Altafjord in Norway late on Christmas Day. They were in pursuit of JW55B and the returning

RA55A, having observed both by long-distance reconnaissance aircraft. British intelligence had cracked the German Navy's Enigma code, so the Allies knew about the German plans.

Battle was joined on Boxing Day. The two forces of large Allied warships closed towards the *Scharnhorst*. The latter despatched her destroyers to attack the outgoing convoy, but thankfully the position given was incorrect, and the merchant ships were not to be found. At nine that morning, the warships of Force 1 opened fire on *Scharnhorst*, which shot back. Early on, *Scharnhorst's* radar was knocked out. In the ensuing battle, with Force 2 joining in the attack, the German ship was at a disadvantage as she could only fire at visible targets, while her opponents could still aim with the aid of radar, from a greater distance.

Scharnhorst scored hits on the *Duke of York* and the *Norfolk*, but was heavily outnumbered and outgunned. Eventually, seriously damaged, she was finished off by torpedoes from four British destroyers. She sank at 7.45 that night with more than one thousand nine hundred men. All her officers perished, and only thirty-six of her crew survived. The outgoing and returning convoys, including Harry's ship, escaped attack from any German units in this battle.

Harry's convoy continued with no further disruption. On 18 February, Harry returned to the UK, and was once again assigned to *HMS President III*.

December 1943 saw Basil Barber at 1651 Heavy Conversion Unit, at Waterbeach in Cambridgeshire, transferring onto four-engined Short Stirling aircraft. He would have known that he was likely soon to be assigned to a squadron taking part in the 'Battle of Berlin', a bombing campaign against Germany's capital city.

The campaign caused heavy casualties to Bomber Command aircrew. To get to Germany, most bombers travelled over occupied countries like Denmark, the Netherlands, Belgium, or France, where many German night fighters and anti-aircraft guns were based. The bombers had to run the gauntlet of these even before they braved the defences over Germany itself.

Since the rapid expansion of the RAF's bomber fleet and the adoption of four-engined bombers, the British bombing campaign had risen in effectiveness. In the early years, many post-raid reports merely stated that the aircraft had bombed a town, or city the crew 'believed to be' Magdeburg, Dusseldorf and so on. Things had changed. Long range navigation beams were capable of putting the bombers over the correct city. There would be hundreds of bombers, seeking to perform 'area bombing,' or 'carpet bombing' as referred to earlier.

The squadrons themselves were now quite large, comprising twenty-five to thirty aircraft, compared to a fighter squadron which would have twelve to eighteen. As bombers would have a larger crew than fighters, the total number of aircrew in a bomber squadron was considerable. Fighter squadrons would be led by squadron leaders, whose rank is the equivalent of an army major. Bomber squadrons on the other hand, were led by wing commanders, the equivalent of an army lieutenant-colonel. The picture below, showing the members of one squadron posing on a Lancaster bomber, gives some idea of the numbers involved.

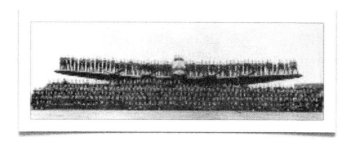

MEMBERS OF 460 SQUADRON WITH LANCASTER
BOMBER 'G FOR GEORGE',
RAF BINBROOK, APRIL 1943.
(Australian War Memorial)

The aim of these large-scale raids was to use incendiary bombs to create a firestorm, destroying the targeted area of a town or city. British bombers carried out such attacks by night, while US bombers now based in Britain, attacked by day.

On 30/31 March 1942 the RAF carried out their first thousand-bomber raid on a German city – Cologne, an important industrial centre. Damage was extensive, although no firestorm was caused. Similar large scale raids would be carried out on other German cities over the coming years. These raids would often cause significant civilian casualties, sometimes in horrific circumstances. In a raid on the port of Hamburg on 27 July 1943, about eight hundred RAF aircraft caused a severe firestorm, devastating huge areas of the city. The concentrated heat caused the tar in some streets to burst into flames. Ground fatalities caused over the four nights of that series of raids on Hamburg exceeded 42,000, most occurring on the night of the 27th.

These attacks fuelled German propaganda, in which bomber aircrew were referred to as 'terror fliers' and 'air gangsters.' Pilots and their crews hoped that if they were shot down, this would happen over occupied countries where the resistance organisations might help them evade capture and return to the UK. They knew that if they came down in Germany they ran a risk of being attacked, perhaps fatally, by angry local civilians or servicemen.

In the US and UK, on the other hand, Harris's efforts were popular. He was seen to be striking back against the enemy, and also to be weakening Germany in the prelude to an invasion of the European mainland. The cover of the US magazine *Time* for June 7 1943 shows a portrait of Harris, against a backdrop showing hammer blows raining upon a swastika.

Not all the attacks were as effective as those on Hamburg and Cologne. In March 1944, Harris launched a large-scale attack on the iconic city of Nuremburg, the scene of famous pre-war Nazi rallies. The raid caused little damage, and the RAF lost about a hundred planes. Five hundred and fifty aircrew were killed, more than the RAF's entire losses during the Battle of Britain. And as in Britain, the morale of the German civilians proved surprisingly resilient. People continued to live their lives as normally as they could despite the frequent attacks.

As Basil approached the end of his training, there was a dispute at the height of British strategic thinking about how to conduct the air war. Harris thought that if he continued to devastate German cities, that country's ability to wage war would be ground down and an enemy surrender was inevitable. On the other hand, the Allied army commanders, who were building up large forces in Britain to invade France the following year wanted him to switch his efforts to bombing transport links in France and elsewhere in the occupied territories, the 'Transportation Strategy', to limit German troop movements when the Allies made their planned landings there.

Despite pressure on Harris from Army generals to follow such a strategy, he persisted in bombing German cities. In November 1943, the heavy raids on Berlin started. From the beginning, damage and casualties in the city were low. The city was well spread out, with wide boulevards, so incendiaries were unlikely to cause firestorms. Also the city was very far away, and well-defended by fighter squadrons and anti-aircraft guns. Even when airmen managed to get to 'The Big City' as aircrew nicknamed it, and drop their bombs, they knew that they had a long trip home, facing German air defences again.

Bomber Command's casualties were high. One Article Fifteen squadron, the Royal Australian Air Force (RAAF) 460 Squadron, lost twenty-five Lancaster aircraft in raids on Berlin from December 1943 to February 1944. This meant that almost the entire strength of the squadron was wiped out and replaced within a few months. With seven men on each aircraft, and many planes crashing over enemy territory, the number of men lost was great.

The aircrew themselves had to survive a tour of duty - thirty missions – before they would be entitled to a transfer to other duties, for example as instructors. Then they would be eligible, but not compelled, to apply for another bombing tour.

SIR ARTHUR 'BOMBER' HARRIS
(Crown Copyright)

Elsewhere, the ground campaign in Europe continued on both fronts. While Eric Priest remained in North Africa, much of the British force which had played a part in defeating the *Afrika Korps* were now in Italy. The capture of Sicily had been followed by the dismissal and later arrest of Mussolini by the King of Italy on 25 July 1943, also an Allied landing at Salerno on the Italian mainland on 3 September 1943. On the latter date, the new Italian government agreed an armistice with the Allies. However, any idea that enemy resistance would soon end was quickly dispelled. German forces continued to resist the Allies, also disarming any Italian soldiers serving alongside them. Mussolini was rescued by German paratroopers within weeks of his arrest. He then led a German-backed government in the north of the country. Meanwhile, the main Italian government switched sides on 13 October 1943, declaring war on Germany.

In late March 1944, after another spell attached to shore establishments, Harry finally got to cross the Atlantic. The trip across the Atlantic was the main supply route for the UK, bringing war material from the US as well as troop reinforcements from the US and Canada. Earlier in the war losses on these routes had been severe- the height of the 'Battle of the Atlantic'. However with improved anti-submarine technology, and considerable coverage by aircraft from both sides of the crossing, the attacks were now far less frequent. U-Boat activity in the Atlantic had declined significantly since autumn of 1943

Harry sailed with the refrigerated-freight ship *Empire Abbey*, which sailed from Liverpool to New York and back. The ship had only recently been launched and seems to have sailed outwards on its own, carrying ballast. *Abbey* seems to have spent almost three weeks - from 7 to 24 April - in New York before joining a convoy for the return trip. Harry and his shipmates would have enjoyed the bright lights of New York, and its rationing-free environment.

Abbey seems to have been a fairly fast ship, hence she was part of the HX convoy series, made up of ships that could achieve speeds of nine to thirteen knots. Her trip back was part of Convoy HX 290 and seems to have passed without incident. After arriving at Liverpool on 14 May, *Abbey* set out again on 8 June, arriving back in New York a little over two weeks later. After another fortnight spent there, she set off back to Liverpool, arriving there on 24 July. Harry remained part of her crew throughout.

Following the surrender of the *Afrika Korps* Eric's service in North Africa had been away from combat zones. He had a week's leave in Egypt in the run-up to Christmas 1943. However, the Italy campaign was not going as well as had been expected. Allied forces were bogged down in the battle against German forces for the ruined monastery of Monte Cassino. An attempt to go round the German defensive lines by landing troops at Anzio had not led to a breakthrough. The battlefront beckoned, and March 1944 saw Eric Priest arrive in Italy, attached initially to 683 Mobile Ambulance Company.

At the start of 1944 Basil went through the final stages of training. On New Year's Day he was transferred to RAF Stradishall in Suffolk, where No. 1651 Heavy Conversion Unit was based, also using Stirling bombers. Basil was assigned to that unit. At the end of the following month he would move to RAF Lindholme in Yorkshire, to Heavy Conversion Unit 1656 which, crucially, flew Avro Lancaster bombers, the sort which most front line squadrons were operating following the replacement of the older Stirlings. Basil was apparently only to have less than a month's flying time on Lancasters before he was assigned to an operational squadron.

On 24 March 1944, Basil was assigned to No. 460 Squadron (RAAF), an Australian Article Fifteen unit based at RAF Binbrook at Caistor in Lincolnshire. As we have seen, 460 Squadron had been involved in the Battle of Berlin, and had suffered heavy losses. Basil would have arrived at the base with an intake of replacement aircrew.

At thirty-five, Basil would have been on the older side for a bomber crew member. Two of his fellow new arrivals were also British, and were much younger. These were air gunners John Septimus Pyne from Oxfordshire, and John Lowes Crouch from Hertfordshire, both of them also Sergeants. Pyne was aged only nineteen, Crouch twenty. Pyne had a family history in the air force – his uncle Reginald had been serving with the Royal Flying Corps and later the RAF, since the first world war, and was at this time an Air Commodore.

Two young Australians already serving with the squadron provide examples of repeated missions and high casualty rates. One was a pilot, Horton Douglas Marsh, who had joined the RAAF as a nineteen-year-old pilot officer months before war broke out. He had been rapidly promoted, becoming a Wing Commander at the start of 1944. He had taken command of the squadron in mid-January, days after his twenty-fourth birthday. While Marsh was an excellent pilot and leader – he would be awarded the Distinguished Flying Cross later in the year – rapid promotions in Bomber Command were, at least in part, a side effect of the high casualty rates. His predecessor but one was by then a prisoner of war, and a later commanding officer would be killed in a mission over Germany before the year was out. Each of those men had led the squadron for about a month before being shot down.

WING COMMANDER HORTON DOUGLAS MARSH,
Basil's CO at 460 SQUADRON
(Australian War Memorial)

The other was Flight Sergeant Ronald Mansfield ('Ron'), a twenty-two year old radio operator. From New South Wales, he had worked in a brick-making factory before the war, joining the RAAF in October 1941. Arriving in the UK in January 1943, he had been assigned to the squadron on 12 December in that year, when the Battle of Berlin was at its height. Days later, on the night of 16 December, he flew on a mission to bomb Berlin. On the return flight the following morning, the Lancaster crashed in the countryside near the airfield, killing the rear gunner. Ron escaped serious injury unlike some of his surviving colleagues. A little over a month later, on 21 January 1944, Ron went on a mission to bomb Magdeburg in Germany. Again, the mission itself was a success, but the plane came down near Caistor on the flight back the following morning. This time no-one was killed, but Ron's injuries were such that his family in Australia were notified of his being wounded.

As Basil and the two Johns were emptying their kit-bags and finding their quarters at Binbrook, the RAF's bombing campaign over Berlin was coming to an end. Harris had finally been directed to switch the bulk of his operations to the 'Transportation Plan'. This would involve air raids aimed at targets chosen to disrupt Germany's ability to reinforce its troops in Northern France in the event of a planned Allied invasion. Targets were likely to include railway junctions, bridges and marshalling yards, mostly in France. Morale in the squadrons was increased by this – one author indicates that the men considered their chances of living into old age to have increased! However, they would still have to carry out some missions into German airspace – Bomber Command also did little-known 'gardening' missions to lay mines in the Baltic Sea off Germany's eastern coast, and these would continue despite the invasion preparations.

Binbrook itself was an older, pre-war airfield, unlike many of the others which had sprouted up all over East Anglia and nearby to host Bomber Command and US Army Air Force squadrons. However, by this time it would be accommodating far more airmen and officers than it would have been before the war. The quarters that many of the crew members would have lived in were quite austere. Airmen were housed in Nissen huts with little heating.

British airmen and officers were a minority in the Australian squadrons, and that situation was normally reflected in the crews. British service-men arriving there would find themselves facing some sort of leg-pulling by their Australian com-rades-in-arms. The tale is told of an English flight engineer being 'initiated' by his Australian crew mates by being soaked under a shower in full uniform, as the Australians 'held the erro-neous view that Englishmen did not wash. After the joshing they all got on famously.' [44]

Basil and his fellow new arrivals did not fly a combat mission for a little over two weeks. A week or so after their arrival, the squadron took part in the disastrous Nuremberg raid, in which twenty-four of their aircraft took part and three did not return. From the lost aircraft, only four men survived to be taken prisoner. This, the rest of the squadron may have hoped, would be the last hurrah for the costly big-city Germany mis-sions.

---

[44] *The Lancaster Men: The Aussie Heroes of Bomber Command* by Peter Rees.

On 9 April 1944, Basil was assigned to the crew of Lancaster bomber ME-727 for a combat flight that night. It would be the squadron's first operational mission since the Nuremberg raid. Twelve of their bombers would be setting out that night to lay mines off the German coast. However three planes, including Basil's, would be joining aircraft from other squadrons in bombing a railway junction at Villeneuve-St-Georges, near Paris.

For most of his crew, this would be the first combat flight. The two Johns were also part of the crew, Pyne in the rear gun turret and Crouch in the mid-upper one. The others were Australians, all at this stage bearing the Flight Sergeant rank, one higher than that of the British members. The pilot, William McKenzie, was a twenty-six-year-old farm hand from Victoria. The navigator was twenty-one year-old Walter Weekes, a university student from New South Wales, and the bomb aimer was Byron Simpson, a twenty-seven-year-old dispensing chemist, also from New South Wales. Byron was the only other married crew member. Lastly, the wireless operator was the one person on board with combat flight experience – the veteran flyer, Ron, for whom this would be the ninth mission.

ME 727 took off at 9.24 that night. The other two bombers from 460 taking part in the Vil-

117

leneuve-St-Georges attack had already taken off almost half an hour before, with planes heading off on the mine-laying operation in between. Almost immediately after take-off, the Lancaster dropped its left wing. It carried out a turn to the left with its wing still down. The bomber continued to turn six complete circles further away from the airfield, losing height and turning even steeper to the left. Eventually, six minutes after take-off, the bomber crashed in Swallow's Wood, about a mile and a half from the airfield, and burned out. Tragically, Basil and all his crew-mates were killed.

All the bombers - from 460 and others units - which bombed Villeneuve-St Georges that night returned safely. But it was a costly night as three of the bombers which went on the mine-laying mission failed to return, with only three of the missing men surviving to be taken prisoner'

The two Johns [45] and the Australian crew

---

[45] The Pyne family were soon to suffer further tragedy, as Air Commodore Pyne was also killed in an air crash, on 17 May.

members,[46] were buried at Cambridge City Cemetery. However, Basil was brought home to Acocks Green, and buried in St Mary's churchyard on 14 April. Gordon Anthony reflects that as his mother Gladys was at the time a Sunday school teacher at the church, she may have had some influence in this matter. Owing to the mutilating effects of the crash, the coffin had to be closed throughout. The Reverend Philip Kelly, who had married Basil and Gladys in 1937, signed the burial register, so it seems he may have officiated at the funeral.

That summer saw significant developments on all fronts. The RAF continued with the Transportation Plan, bombing railways, bridges and other installations, mostly in Northern France. The Soviet Army swept further westwards, entering Poland. The Polish resistance movement rose up against the German forces and seized the capital Warsaw, hoping to re-establish the authority of the pre-war Polish government. However the Soviet army halted its advance until the uprising had been defeated, seeking to establish a communist government in Poland af-

---

[46] The following month all RAAF pilots flying as captain on four engine aircraft were promoted to officer rank. (Rees, op cit above).This seems to have resulted in William McKenzie receiving a posthumous promotion to Pilot Officer.

ter the war. After crushing the rebellion, the Germans largely destroyed the city.

Following the North African campaign General Montgomery - 'Monty' - had continued his leadership role. He had led Allied forces in Sicily and on the Italian mainland, and was expected to do likewise in the planned invasion of France. British intelligence decided to use a 'double' posing as him to spread false intelligence about the proposed invasion. The double, Lieutenant Meyrick E Clifton-James, was an officer from the Royal Army Pay Corps based at Leicester! He had come to prominence in that city by appearing on stage at De Montfort Hall dressed as Monty. Gordon may have known him from work, or from his stage appearances.[47]   After the war, Clifton-James's story was told in the book and film, 'I Was Monty's Double.'

---

[47] BBC Website: 'WW2: People's War', Ada Poland
BBC 'People's War,', submitted 21 October 2004
http://www.bbc.co.uk/history/ww2peopleswar/stories/18/a3162818.shtml

LT M E CLIFTON JAMES IN DISGUISE AS
MONTY(left), MONTY HIMSELF AT RIGHT
(both Crown Copyright)

On 6 June 1944, British, American, Canadian,
Free French and other Allied forces landed in
Normandy, bringing about the main Second
Front. The Allied campaign in Italy, which had
seized the public's attention only the day before
with the capture of Rome, now faded from view,
even though it was as keenly fought as before.
Elation in Britain at the successful landings in
France was tempered by news that the home
front was under attack again. Shortly after the
invasion, Germany had started to fire V1 'flying
bombs' – pilotless missiles similar to small jet
planes – mostly aimed at London. These caused
heavy casualties there, but the people of Birmingham and other cities north of London
breathed a sigh of relief that this weapon was

unlikely to affect them as seemed to be out of its range.

Meanwhile, Harry went to sea in the *Empire Abbey* again. On 9 August the ship set sail from Liverpool, heading for Latin America. *Abbey* reached Buenos Aires, Argentina, on 13 September, and called at Montevideo, the capital of Uruguay, almost a couple of weeks later.

Chapter Five: The Final Stretch

In the Far East, Allied forces were continuing their successes against the Japanese. In September 1943, British and Australian commandos had struck in the harbour of Japanese-occupied Singapore, sinking seven ships with no loss to themselves. However, as the Allies did not then publicise how the sabotage was carried out, the Japanese assumed that the attack was the work of locally-based resistance fighters. Accordingly, in October the secret police force, the Kempetei, rounded up many Singapore residents on suspicion of involvement. Those arrested were detained for lengthy periods, and tortured. One of the detainees was the Bishop of Singapore, John Leonard Wilson, who features later on in this work.

A Japanese invasion of India from Burma was defeated by British and Indian forces in the battles of Imphal and Kohima, in March-July 1944. Further east, American forces were making progress in their campaigns to capture islands from the Japanese. In June 1944 they captured the island of Saipan, providing a base for air raids against Japan.

Meanwhile, Japan's own plans to build a working airfield on Haruku were being wound down. From October 1943 onwards, the Japanese began to ship the sick, or rather most sickprisoners of war back to Java. This in itself sadly led to tragedy. One such draft was on the ship *Suez Maru* on 29 November 1943, which – unmarked with any Red Cross, or other relevant markings - was torpedoed and sunk by a US submarine, with heavy loss of life. Dennis was apparently in better health than many of the other prisoners, and so he was not put on any of the sick draft ships.

From May 1944 onwards, the relatively healthy prisoners were moved off Haruku as well.[48] They were, of course, transported on 'hellships' which were in poor condition. As on the trip out, the ships were heavily overcrowded. On 17 September, the *Maros Maru* (also known as the *Hariyoshi Maru*) left Haruku with five hundred prisoners on board, headed for Batavia (Java). Dennis was one of those boarding.

The journey was to last sixty-seven days, although it covered a relatively short distance as we have seen. The *Maros Maru* was an old Dutch ship, scuttled at the start of the occupation, then salvaged and refloated by the Japanese. The prisoners were provided with very little

---

[48] *Unsung Heroes of the RAF*, (2002) Pam and Les Stubbs, Barny Books, pp 56-60.

food or water. The ship made many stops, picking up large numbers of additional prisoners, till they totalled about six hundred and fifty. As the ship was so overcrowded, many of the prisoners were on the deck, clad (if at all) in rags and so inadequately dressed for shelter from the harsh tropical sun. Sickness seems to have broken out swiftly – dysentery and beriberi among other illnesses.

The Japanese officers and non-commissioned officers treated the prisoners as brutally afloat as they did on shore, with beatings being given for any offence. Punishment could even be by proxy – a prisoner fell into the sea while trying to relieve himself, and though the Japanese turned the ship round and saved the prisoner, the Allied officers and non-commissioned officers on board were beaten as a punishment for letting this incident happen. [49]

On 29 September the ship stopped at Celebes with an engine fault. Eventually some of the Royal Navy prisoners undertook the repairs, which took some time. The ship restarted after four days. However, the hardships on board

---

[49] COFEPOW (Children of Far East Prisoners of War) website, chapter *The Maros Maru,* https://www.cofepow.org.uk/armed-forces-stories-list/the-maros-maru.

were taking their toll, with a high death rate. The dead would be tied into sacks, weighted with sandbags, and dropped into the sea after the Burial Service was read over them. Dennis, it seems, was now ill with bacillary dysentery. During the layover at Celebes, thirty-six men had died.

On 3 October, six more men succumbed. Sadly, Dennis was among them. Along with other dead prisoners, he was buried at sea. He had served with the RAF since shortly after the outbreak of war, had been a prisoner of the Japanese for two-and-a-half years, and had been on Haruku for a year and a half. He had the distinction of having served against all of Britain's main World War Two adversaries, Italy, Germany, Vichy France and Japan.

The suffering of his fellow prisoners was to continue, as the ship was to make another, even longer delay, tied up at Macassar for about forty days during which there were hundreds more deaths. When the ship eventually arrived at mainland Java, almost half of the prisoners had died.

As Dennis lay dying, another of our subjects was also gravely ill - although perhaps in less harrowing circumstances, and thousands of miles away. Gordon Helm was suffering from tuberculosis, and was admitted at the Isolation

Hospital in Leicester. Tragically, he too passed away, two days after Dennis's death. Gordon was buried at St Mary's ten days later, in his mother's grave. Like Basil before him, he was apparently buried by the same man who had officiated at his wedding, the Reverend Philip Kelly.

LEICESTER ISOLATION HOSPITAL
(Historic England)

Harry was at sea at the time, still with *Empire Abbey*, having sailed from Liverpool on 9 August. He had arrived at Buenos Aires on 25 September, and at Montevideo the following day. The ship then headed back across the Atlantic, arriving at Freetown, Sierra Leone on 15 October, where they stayed for three days. He returned to the UK with *Abbey*, on 7 November 1944. Harry was transferred briefly to a shore establishment (*HMS President III* again) from 8 to 14 November 1944, then back to *Abbey* which was in UK waters at the time, undergoing repairs. It may well be that the transfer to *President* was to allow him to take compassionate leave in the aftermath of his brother's death. On his return to *Abbey*, he remained assigned to her until the repairs were completed at Newport, Gwent on 22 November. Harry was then assigned to the DEMS unit based at Newport, and shortly afterwards to the one at Cardiff.

As the year wore on, Eric remained with ambulance units in Italy, where the fighting against German and pro-Mussolini Italian forces made slow progress. The public back home took more interest in the French campaign, where Allied forces had broken out of the Normandy beachhead and liberated Paris in August. Other Allied forces also invaded the south of France, and headed northwards. By early September 1944 Allied forces were in Belgium and the Netherlands. Later that month British, American and Polish paratroopers landed behind German lines in the Netherlands in 'Operation Market Garden', seeking to capture crucial bridges enabling a crossing over the Rhine and a swift invasion of Germany itself. Sadly the airborne attacks turned out to be, literally, 'a bridge too far,' and the operation failed following the defeat of British troops at Arnhem. Despite this, and a German counterattack in the Ardennes at Christmas 1944, the Allied advance continued.

Birmingham – along with other cities north of London - held its breath shortly before Christmas 1944, when the threat of air attack returned. The V-1 flying bomb was normally unable to reach so far north. However in late 1944 German bombers carrying V-1s flew over the North Sea and launched their weapons. On Christmas Eve a number of them launched V-1s aimed at Manchester, but they hit a number of different targets. One landed in Oldham, Lancashire, causing thirty-four deaths. Birmingham was not hit, although one such bomb landed in Newport, Shropshire less than forty miles away thankfully, causing no casualties and limited damage [50]. Many of the German bombers were shot down in these attacks, and they soon ceased. V-1 – and later the much faster V-2 rocket bomb – would continue to strike London and other southern targets.

The New Year also brought Eric Priest – still serving in Italy - a promotion to Lance Corporal. Allied progress continued on all fronts. Soviet forces entered the ruins of the Polish capital Warsaw. This brought them closer to the borders of Germany proper, although this also meant

---

[50] *Newport's War, A History of a Shropshire Market Town Between 1939-1948*, by Malcolm Miles.

that Poland would be ruled by pro-Soviet communists after the war, rather than by the non-communists of the London-based government-in-exile. In the Far East, General Slim's multinational force pushed back the Japanese in Burma, with soldiers from Britain, Australia, India, West and East Africa all playing their part. March brought good news - Allied forces crossed the Rhine into Germany, following the seizure of the bridge at Remagen on the 7th. But for one of our subjects, the month was to bring yet more tragedy.

William Frederick Helm, Great War veteran and father of Gordon and Harry, passed away on 17 March, at Selly Oak Hospital, from arteriosclerosis. Harry was at another shore establishment, and was apparently given some time in which to deal with this latest bereavement. He appears on the death certificate as informant. William was buried with his wife and elder son in the St Mary's churchyard.

As the war came to its close, much of the remaining action came in the air. Following the invasion of Normandy and its immediate aftermath, the attacks on Germany's cities had resumed. In February 1945 came the mission that was to greatly affect the reputation of RAF's Bomber Command and their American counterparts. Hundreds of British bombers struck at the eastern German city of Dresden on the nights of

13 and 14 February, with American aircraft striking on the following days. The city was supposedly targeted for its railway junctions and other transport infrastructure. Many of the bombs used were incendiary, and they caused a firestorm. Casualties, mostly civilian, were high. Over 20,000 people were killed, and the city was largely destroyed. However, the Nazi authorities claimed that between 100,000 and 200,000 people had died in the attacks, and this figure was widely repeated. The British prime minister, Winston Churchill, until then a strong supporter of Harris's strategy, issued a memo which contained the following comments:

'It seems to me that the moment has come when the question of bombing of German cities simply for the sake of increasing the terror, though under other pretexts, should be reviewed. Otherwise we shall come into control of an utterly ruined land. The destruction of Dresden remains a serious query against the conduct of Allied bombing. I feel the need for more precise concentration upon military objectives such as oil and communications behind the immediate battle-zone, rather than on mere acts of terror and wanton destruction, however impressive.'[51]

---

[51] *Bomber Boys* (2007)by Patrick Bishop, Harper Perennial p.362.

Churchill was to withdraw the memo later, but the damage was done. Britain's war leader had implicitly called his own and other Allied airmen 'terror fliers,' and the supposed figures of hundreds of thousands of dead in Dresden took root all over the world.

Meanwhile, the Allied campaign in Italy was making progress. Forces from Britain, the US, Free France, and many other nations including the Polish government-in-exile, Greece and Brazil, pushed northwards, with the help of an uprising by Italian partisan resistance fighters. On 1 April 1945, Eric suffered an injury while getting out of an ambulance. It must have been sufficiently serious to be marked in his service record, his superiors making it clear that the injury occurred on duty and that he was not to blame. Thankfully he seems to have made a full recovery.

The Italian campaign ended on May 2 1945, with the surrender of German forces there. Mussolini's Nazi-backed state had already been routed, and he had been seized and lynched by partisans late in April.

Meanwhile the Western Allies and the Soviet forces pushed deeper and deeper into Germany itself. Concentration camps in the West and East were liberated, with their severely emaciated inmates finally regaining their freedom. The

German government finally surrendered unconditionally a few days later, on 7 May, following
the suicide of Hitler as Soviet forces closed in on
his bunker in Berlin.

The end of the war in Europe had an immediate consequence in Britain. Although her
forces were still fighting Japan in the Far East, a
general election was called for July 1945 and
the wartime national government was on its way
out. Clement   Attlee's Labour Party won by a
landslide, and Churchill and his Conservative
Party went into opposition.

Eric Priest had by now been abroad for more
than three years. With the war in Europe coming
to an end, he was granted a brief spell of leave
in the UK. As his leave was only from 15 to 23
July 1945, it is likely he was flown out of Italy to
Britain and back. This was under the LIAP
scheme under which any serviceman who had
served overseas, and was ultimately to be demobilised, was given a short home leave.[52]

In the Far East the Japanese had been driven
out of much of the territory that they had occupied. Their government refused to surrender,
however, even after being warned by the US and

[52] BBC Website: 'WW2: People's War,' James Glew,
submitted 14 November 2003, www.bbc.co.uk/history/
ww2peopleswar/stories/57/a2008757.shtml.

other Allies of the risk of 'the utter devastation of the Japanese homeland.'[53] American bomber aircraft duly dropped atomic bombs on the Japanese cities of Hiroshima and Nagasaki on August 6 and 9 respectively. These caused hundreds of thousands of deaths, and great devastation. Japan surrendered unconditionally on 15 August 1945.

The war was over, although it left many more troubles in its wake.

---

[53] Ultimatum issued by Allied leaders at the Potsdam Conference, held in occupied Germany 17 July to 2 August 1945

Chapter Six: Aftermath

One consequence of the end of hostilities was the liberation of Allied prisoners of war. The reverse was not the case - German and other Axis prisoners of the Allies were detained for months, or even years afterwards. The Soviet Union detained such prisoners for up to ten years as a source of labour. It is not so well known that Britain kept German and Italian prisoners of war on UK soil for the same reason, for up to three years, the last being repatriated towards the end of 1948.

Allied prisoners in the West had been in contact with their families through letters sent by the Red Cross, so those relatives would have already known that their family members were still alive. But as we have seen the Japanese did not observe such rules of international law. Many relatives of men captured in the Far East had no idea whether their relatives had been captured alive or, like the Barbers, they only had dated information.

Thankfully, British and other prisoners of the Japanese kept meticulous records of deaths in custody, even though such record-keeping could have cost them their own lives if the Japanese had discovered their notes. The details of those who perished on the *Maros Maru* show clearly who died on which day, and death certificates later issued show that the specific cause of death was recorded too. It is likely that the Barber family learnt of Dennis's death within a few months of the end of the war in the Far East.

Harry Helm was apparently serving at a shore establishment, *HMS Vernon*, when the war ended. However, he was then assigned to a sea-going Royal Navy ship for the first time in his career. Between August and December 1945 he served on the frigate *HMS Spragge*, which was sent to serve with the Pacific Fleet following the Japanese surrender. *Spragge* sailed to Hong Kong and Singapore. She was then handed over to United States forces in the Philippines, having been supplied to Britain by the Americans under a lend-lease scheme. Harry and his crew-mates presumably returned home on other ships.

Harry was to stay in the Navy, however, until April 1946, his last attachment being to *HMS Victory* for some six months. It is not clear whether he was actually based on that vessel – Admiral Nelson's old flagship, in dry dock at Portsmouth – or whether he was just on the books there for administrative reasons.

Eric Priest, also happily survived the war. He remained in Italy until his return to the UK on 31 December 1945. Shortly before he left Italy, his superior officer gave him the following glowing reference:

'The NCO has always carried out his duties conscientiously and willingly, and I have always found him honest and trustworthy.'

Like Harry, he stayed in the forces until de-mobilisation in April 1946.

All over Western Europe former Nazi officials, and their local collaborators, were being rounded up and brought to trial for their crimes. A similar situation was unfolding in the Far East, where Allied prisoners had recently been freed from the brutal conditions in the Japanese prisoner of war camps. Some of the former Allied prisoners were to volunteer as war crimes investigators. This led to a role reversal, where some former prisoners found themselves taking their former tormentors into custody.

One example was Wing Commander Pitts, who as a Squadron Leader had been a senior British officer on Haruku while Dennis Barber was held there. Pitts was to take into custody Sergeant-Major Mori, at whose hands he had suffered in the past, and also Mori's interpreter Kasiyama as well as the former camp commander Kurashima. In 1946, all these men were to face a war crimes trial in Singapore, along with others including the Japanese colonel Anami –

the man known as 'Whiskers,' who had been in overall charge of the camps including Haruku.

The charges they faced included the ill-treatment of prisoners on Ambon and Haruku, the atrocity of the *Maros Maru* featuring prominently. Most of the accused Japanese and Koreans, including those mentioned above, were found guilty. Mori, Kurashima and Anami were condemned to death and hanged. The interpreter Kasiyama was sentenced to life imprisonment. In the event he was not to serve long – he was released to work for the western Allies as an interpreter in his native Korea when another war broke out there a few years later.

BACK ROW: WING COMMANDER PITTS AND AN
UNKNOWN BRITISH SERVICEMAN.
FRONT ROW l to r: KURASHIMA, KASIYAMA and
MORI (Anon, from *Prisoners in Java*).

Post-war Britain was simultaneously hopeful and exhausted. The new government established the National Health Service, and embarked on large-scale house-building to replace the stock lost in air raids and flying bomb attacks. In particular, Birmingham saw the building of new housing estates at Druids Heath, Castle Vale and Bromford within the city boundaries, and at Chelmsley Wood just outside. Some rationing was still in force, and so many of the day to day hardships of the wartime era continued. Despite the hard-won peace, the prospect of another war, this time against the Soviet Union and its communist allies, loomed large.

Both of the surviving Priest brothers who had served in the regular forces were to marry shortly after the war. Alec married Louise Stebbings at a registry office in Fulham on 21 December 1946. Eric married Doreen Tomkins on 20 September 1947, at the parish church in Sheldon. Both men were eventually to live in the south of England, Alec in Sussex and Eric in Hampshire. From the marriage certificates, both men were working as drivers.

Harry, meanwhile, was employed by Whitbread Brewery, and was to work at their factories at Luton and London. He married Ellen Shortiss in Ealing on 15 February 1947. They had a daughter, Susan, in 1949.

On 6 September 1950, Frederick Priest Senior, Great War veteran and father of the Priest brothers, passed away from heart failure and bronchitis. Elsie Gwendola, his widow, was also to die a few years later, on 16 January 1954, from heart disease.

In 1951, a peace treaty was signed between Japan and the Allies. One provision of the agreement was that Japanese assets could be seized, and another provided that compensation could be paid to former prisoners. In Birmingham, an advertisement was put in the *Birmingham Mail* for names of Far East prisoners to be submitted. Almost a thousand names were given, Annie Barber sending in Dennis's name. Far East ex-prisoner of war associations were strongly supported in Birmingham by the Anglican bishop of the city, John Leonard Wilson, a former civilian detainee from his time as Bishop of Singapore. He served as the inaugural patron of Birmingham's association of Far East Prisoners of War.

As we have seen, the peace that followed the war proved deceptive. Britain found itself embroiled in conflict with communist and nationalist insurgents in many of its territories – Palestine, Malaya, Cyprus and Kenya among others. India, Pakistan, Burma and many other colonies won their independence from Britain.

In 1950 came the long-anticipated clash between the Western powers and the Communist world– North Korea, which was Communist, invaded South Korea, which was an American client state. The United Nations rallied round the South, sending thousands of troops to repel the invasion. Most were American, but a significant number of British troops and those of other nations, were committed to this war. The war ended in stalemate after three years– the border between the two Koreas remained and remains more or less where it had been at the start. Many former British service personnel, including many World War II veterans, had been called up again, and sent eastwards to serve in this conflict. Thankfully, neither of the surviving Priest brothers nor Harry was recalled in this way.

To keep a flow of much-needed recruits into the military, Britain retained conscription till well after the Second World War. The late 1950s found conscription, or 'national service' as it was known, still in force although soon to be abolished. Hence young men whose fathers, or mothers had served in the Second World War could well be called up in their turn. However, Gordon Anthony Barber finished school later than anticipated. As a result, he just missed the last national service call-up – there were no more conscripts in the British armed forces after 1962. The Barbers, having suffered so grievously during the War, were spared further military jeopardy. In September 1968, Annie Sophia Barber, mother to Dennis and Basil, passed away at the age of eighty-eight.

The aftermath of tragedy saw one of our subjects drawn back to the military. Eric's wife Doreen sadly died from kidney failure in April 1956, in Queen Alexandra Hospital in Cosham. Five years later, still employed as a driver, Eric rejoined the Territorial Army at Portsmouth. This time he entered the Royal Corps of Signals, serving in 327 Signal Squadron. He remained for three years, attending annual training camps until the end of his service in 1964. His period of service included the Berlin Crisis of 1961 and the Cuba Missile Crisis the following year – two spells of major tension between the Western and Soviet blocs. He may well have feared the possibility of another major war occurring while he was still in uniform.

Frederick Priest Junior passed away at Solihull Hospital on 14 February 1970. The oldest of the Priest brothers, he died twenty-seven years to the day after the passing of the youngest brother, Leslie.

Alec and Louise Priest had four children, two sons and two daughters. By the early 1970s the couple were living in Crawley, Sussex. Sadly, Alec and his family were also to face tragedy. In

1971 his first son died in an accident, aged twenty-one, and the following year, Louise passed away from natural causes.

Both Priest brothers were to remarry. In October 1965, a little over a year after the end of his second spell in the army, Douglas Priest married Phyllis Kelsey, at Saints Peter and Paul Church, Portsmouth. Alec was to marry Lillian Woodnett (herself a widow) at the registry office in Crawley in 1980.

Also in 1980, Sidney's widow, Gladys May Barber passed away. Betsy Helm, Gordon Helm's widow, died in 1992. Neither woman had remarried.

The remaining Priest brothers were to pass away within the space of five years, in the late twentieth century. Alec died at Worthing on 7 January 1988, and Eric – the final surviving Priest sibling - at Portsmouth on 26 November 1992.

Valerie Field, the older sister of Basil and Dennis Barber, died in 1993. The author believes that their younger sister Christine Botherway has also passed away, but has no date of this event.

The last of our subjects, Harry Helm, lived into this decade. He died, aged eighty-nine, in March 2011, his wife having predeceased him eleven years earlier. The Wokingham local paper ran an obituary of him.[54] With interesting symmetry, Gerd Kiebling, captain of the German submarine which nearly claimed Harry's life in the sinking of the *Dafila*, lived to the same age and died five years before Harry's passing.[55]

All but one of our subjects who served and died in the war, are remembered at St Mary The Virgin churchyard in Acocks Green. Gordon Grant Helm, Vernon Leslie Priest, and Sidney Basil Barber are each buried there, under Commonwealth War Graves gravestones. Gordon Helm's gravestone also alludes to the fact that both his parents are buried in the same grave. Leslie's gravestone also commemorates Alf's passing, he is referred to as having been 'lost at sea'. Alf is also commemorated on the Brookwood Memorial, Surrey, which carries the names of thousands of British and Commonwealth war dead who have no known grave.

Dennis Barber is not mentioned on Basil's gravestone or on the war memorial inside the church. However, he is remembered on the war memorial at Kranji in Singapore along with

---

54 Wokingham Times, exact date unknown, April 2009, posted to Get Reading website 14 April 2011.

55 Uboatnet website.

24,000 other Commonwealth casualties whose bodies were not recovered.

All of them, however, are mentioned in the books of war dead contained in Birmingham's Hall of Memory, the striking war memorial located in Centenary Square in the city centre. Not far from St Mary The Virgin church, in front of the village library, is Acocks Green's own war memorial, which does not have individual names on it. The village had not put up such a memorial for the Great War, but after the later conflict the local branch of the British Legion raised funds for a 'Peace Garden', including the memorial to the dead of both wars, which was dedicated in 1965 by the Rev Charles Iball, then the vicar at St Mary's, where he had succeeded the Rev Philip Kelly.

The country honoured the war service of its veterans, living, or dead, by issuing medals and clasps. In addition to medals awarded for acts of bravery, and the medals issued to all who served in the War, 'campaign medals' were issued. Every service member who took part in a specific campaign would be entitled to any campaign medal, or clasp, issued. Where the service member died before the medal could be issued, it would be sent to the next of kin. However, as we shall see, not every campaign was marked by the issue of a medal, or clasp.

RAF officers and airmen who served in the Battle of Britain, defending the country against German bombers and fighters during the summer of 1940, were honoured by the award of a clasp carrying the words 'Battle of Britain' and worn on the 1939-45 Star. However, the men of Bomber Command did not receive similar recognition. This was so despite their extremely high casualty rate – of 125,000 aircrew, 55,573 were killed, with thousands more injured or captured.

This omission was due, in part at least, because the reputation of Bomber Command had suffered in the aftermath of the Dresden raid. In response to the failure to reward his men, 'Bomber' Harris declined the offer of a peerage, the only surviving wartime commander-in-chief to do so. He left the country shortly after the war and worked abroad for some years.

Those who had served on the Arctic convoys were also to suffer a lack of recognition. The reasons there were entirely political. As we have seen, the western Allies fell out with the Soviet Union and most other communist states after the war. It became inconvenient for Western countries to acknowledge that they had supported the Soviet Union, propping it up and saving it from defeat. Like the men of Bomber Command, the sailors of the Arctic convoys had suffered horrendous casualties. Those who had survived the voyages had endured extreme winter weather.

Over many decades, the tide of opinion turned. More historical works were published on the efforts of Bomber Command, and the public came to take a more balanced look at their reputation. The exaggerated casualty figures for the Dresden raid were discredited. Likewise, people became more familiar with the fact that the 'area bombing' policy had originated from political leaders, and not from Harris.

In 1992 a statue of Sir Arthur Harris, who had died eight years earlier, was put up in front of St Clement's Dane, the RAF church on the Strand in London. It was next to the one of Fighter Command's wartime leader Lord Dowding, which had been standing there for some years. Protests were held at the unveiling and the mayors of Hamburg and Dresden expressed their opposition. Despite the controversy, the statue of Harris survived, initially being regularly targeted with graffiti.

Likewise, there was increased interest in the history of the Arctic Convoys. At every Remembrance Sunday parade, television commentators would draw attention to the thinning groups of elderly men wearing their distinctive white berets, and it would be noted that these men had not been acknowledged for their service in the

Arctic. The collapse of the Soviet Union and the fall of the communist regimes in the late 1980s and early 1990s meant that the political reasons for not honouring the Arctic veterans were no longer relevant.

Unfortunately nothing was done about rewarding the Arctic veterans while Harry was still alive. It was at the end of 2012 that the then Prime Minister, David Cameron, announced that a campaign medal would be issued to the Arctic veterans, or their next of kin. It would be known as the Arctic Star. At the same time, a Bomber Command clasp was to be issued to surviving aircrew or their next of kin.

Bomber Command - particularly Basil and his comrades - are also remembered in Australia. The reputation of Bomber Command seems not to have suffered there as much as in the UK and elsewhere. In part this may be because Australia lost so many men in the bombing campaign and so honoured their service. Only 2% of Australians who enlisted during the war flew with Bomber Command, but they provided 20% of her war dead. [56]

460 Squadron was disbanded after the war. However, it was revived in 2010, as a non-flying,

---

[56] *The Lancaster Men: The Aussie Heroes of Bomber Command* by Peter Rees.

intelligence squadron of the RAAF. As the squadron with the highest casualties in the RAAF's bombing campaign, its memory had never been allowed to die. Its banner was, and is, flown at Anzac Day parades, on which Australia and New Zealand commemorate their war dead. The picture below shows such a banner being displayed at a march in Brisbane – the number of casualties is not rounded up or down. Every man lost, British, Australian, or other, is remembered.

460 SQUADRON BANNER AT 2007 ANZAC DAY
PARADE
(www.brisbaneishome)

At the Australian War Memorial in Canberra, Basil and his comrades in arms are remembered, generally and specifically. Generally, the 460 Squadron's Lancaster bomber 'G for George', shown in the squadron group picture on page 105, is displayed as a memorial to the RAAF bomber crew. More specifically, a flying jacket which belonged to Ron Mansfield is also on display. This was the jacket he wore at the time of his second crash, and still shows a tear from that incident. He would have been wearing a different jacket at the time of the crash in which he, Basil and their crew-mates were killed. That crash is referred to in the exhibit.

RON MANSFIELD'S FLYING JACKET,
(the tear is visible at the top of the right sleeve,
at left of picture)
(Australian War Memorial)

It was a long while before Britain constructed a memorial to the men of Bomber Command.
When this was finally put up, in the summer of
2012, it was mostly at private expense. The
memorial stands in Green Park, London, and its
motto is 'Freedom is the sure possession of
those alone who have the courage to defend it.'

ACOCKS GREEN WAR MEMORIAL

"The shall grow not old as we that are left grow old"

Chapter Seven: Postcript

We have reached the end of the journey through the war service of the members of these three families. Each family played their part in this country's darkest hour, and each paid a great price. As far as I can tell, these men did not seek glory. In the Great War, their fathers' generation had mobbed the recruiting offices in a wave of patriotic fervour. Our subjects probably served out of a sense of duty – their country called, and they answered that call. They may even have done so with some trepidation, as they and the whole nation well knew the high price paid in the previous war. And yet they stepped up willingly. In particular, I think of the elder Priest brothers volunteering before their age-group was called up, or of Basil Barber putting himself forward for a combat aircrew role. These were all men who had plans for what they wanted to do in life, in each case the war shattered their plans. Even those who survived had their lives changed forever by the loss of a sibling, or siblings.

I had the honour of being in contact with members of each family over the past few years. What struck me most was how the loss of family members was keenly felt, even by those very young, or not even alive at the time. This is so for families elsewhere, as I was equally privileged to exchange online communications with a family member of Ron Mansfield in Australia.

We may sometimes read of battles in which casualties are 'light'. The fundamental message I drew from encounters and contacts with relatives of the fallen was simply this – as long as anyone is killed in a battle, or suffers life-changing injuries, then there are no light casualties. Those lost by these families are still mourned, more than seventy years after the war ended.

May those who have to take the weighty decision about whether or not to send this country's present-day armed forces into conflict, reflect hard and long on these matters before they make such decisions.

The End

.

Printed in Great Britain
by Amazon